MUSIC: NOW AND THEN

MUSIC:

COLEMAN-ROSS COMPANY, INC.
New York

NOW AND THEN

ASHLEY PETTIS

NIHIL OBSTAT: Rev. William J. Konus
                Censor Librorum

IMPRIMATUR: ✠ John King Mussio
                Bishop of Steubenville

February 25, 1955
Steubenville, Ohio

ML
166
.P4

COPYRIGHT 1955 BY COLEMAN-ROSS COMPANY, INC.

All rights reserved. No part of this book may be reproduced in any form without permission in writing from the publishers. Designed by Mark Fowler. Monotype composition by Northeastern Press. Printed and bound by The Riverside Press.

Manufactured in the
United States of America

To the Rev. Joseph J. McGowan, S. J.
>whose clarion trumpet has called
an untold number to the Mount

Contents

Foreword: DAVID: A MUSICAL MONUMENT	1
Introduction	7
NOW: MUSIC IN OUR TIME	
The Music Industry	9
The Concert Field	10
The Radio Antennae	12
Records	14
Hollywood	15
Opera	16
Orchestral Music	17
Music Education	19
The Juke Box	22

Contemporary Music	22
"Popular" Music	28
Musical Undercurrents	29

THEN: OUR MUSICAL HERITAGE FROM THE BIBLE

Concerning Points of Inquiry	33
A Biblical Preface	35
Use of Single Instruments	36
The *Sound of the Trumpet*	38
Instruments in Combination	51
Women in Biblical Music	54
Song, Without Instruments	59
Abuse of Music; and in Lamentation	63
Song, With Instruments	74
Hymns, Psalms, and Canticles	96

Foreword

⋄ DAVID: A Musical Monument

"Objective" evaluation of musical experience has to do with two factors of importance: (1) the special quality (nature) of reactions *during;* (2) the residuum, *after* the event. The first is primarily "subjective." Objectivity, if attained, derives from the latter. In some instances reactions are so mixed and varied, at the time of occurrence, that the *embarras des richesses*, or otherwise, leaves one in a state of inarticulate wonderment. As this condition is gradually dispelled, subjective chaos is superseded by objective clarity, in which relative values are contemplated in perspective.

The foregoing is merely an introductory approach to a colossal musical monument: *DAVID*, a figure that rises from the welter of Biblical musical references, towering above all other musical figures of antiquity.

It would require the genius and craftmanship of a Michelangelo, properly and adequately to re-create the various contributions of David to our musical traditions, in order to present them to all men, reassembled in integrated form and completeness: *a colossal musical monument.* For such he was and is!

That music historians and musicologists have failed to place David on the pedestal that is rightfully his,

Music: Now and Then

may, but should not, cause surprise. "Ears they have, and they hear not; eyes they have, and they see not," is common, both in high and low places. Many are they who have neither heard "the sound of the trumpet" nor seen David in perspective, although within range of both.

One does not have to search far to find those "authorities" who have failed to credit David with some of the most important, far-reaching contributions, both to the music of his own time as well as to living tradition. The layman, at least, in quest of musical "facts," frequently reaches for that standard reference work, Grove's Dictionary of Music and Musicians. If he turns to the letter "D," in search of "David," he will not find what he is looking for.* Historians and musicologists, generally, have failed to perceive, or have ignored, the *complete* David: performer, organizer, creator, originator of instrumental combinations as well as the expansion of vocal resources, improviser, musical prophet, librettist, prototype of musicians; and, above all, one who established traditions whose antennae extend into musical annals and practices, even to our own day. It seems incredible: but it is true!

As a performer, David is primarily remembered in connection with the occasion of Saul's being in a "slough of despond." The references to David's "skill" (see page 36) might well be taken with a grain of salt, considering the frequent fallibility of critical dicta. But

* Since this was written, Mr. Eric Blom, Editor of the fifth edition of Grove's Dictionary, has included an article on David, written by the author of this book, in that publication.

David: A Musical Monument

the fact that he was chosen to perform for the king, *only after search had been made* for a "man skilful in playing on the harp," seems to be valid enough evidence that he stood up well in comparison with others whose existence is to be assumed. That, after David's playing, "Saul was refreshed, and was better," may be taken as the first clinical report on music therapy, as well as evidence of an indubitably "successful" performance. At any rate, in selection and listener's response, David may be classified safely with those who not only were "called," but "chosen": in other words, placed among the "few."

David's manifold activities in connection with the worship of God form the body of the towering figure, and reveal, as well, the mystic workings of divine spirit. His adventurous nature, by the grace of God, illumined homage to the Almighty through music, in many unprecedented manifestations. These not only included singing, often with greatly expanded resources and instruments of unparalleled diversity, but improvised dancing before the Ark of God (see pages 52, 76–77, 95, 97–98). Although organization of liturgical music was given due consideration, and various members of the Levites were properly assigned to their respective duties (see pages 76–81, 97–98), divine inspiration imbued such occasions with a spirit of improvisation (see pages 52–53, 55–56, 97–99) which not only glorified the worship of God at appointed times and places, but has had far reaching influence even to modern days (see pages 53, 98–99).

The crowning glory of David's musical manifestations was undoubtedly that "spiritual epitome of all mankind," the Psalms (see pages 108–118). That they were indissolubly linked with music in their day, and in varying degrees since but without exact knowledge of David's musical settings, in which he was both composer and performer, is too well known to receive more than passing mention at this point. But their imperishable spirit not only illumines David's musical physiognomy from within, but has lighted and will continue to light the path of faith *ad infinitum*. Even in the absence of David's musical investiture, the Psalms loom as the most extraordinary literary works of any composer-librettist in the annals of history. In their incandescent light, the very consideration of all other poetic emanations of creative musicians vanishes in nothingness. The sun of the splendor of the Psalms cannot be dimmed by invidious comparison.

It did not require the lapse of time to place David's musical contributions and innovations in perspective. His influence was immediately responsible for the establishing of traditions that assured the continuation of liturgical practices, instituted and expanded by him, in that spirit by which he was exalted. There are many later Biblical references that clearly show that he was looked upon by those that came after him as the prototype of musicians (see page 67, *et al.*). The recounting of the practical steps taken to perpetuate David's musical activities, as well as their continued life, form a fascinating tale, particularly when removed from Biblical context (see pages 79–100).

Robert Schumann's *Davidsbund,* in which the spirit

David: A Musical Monument

of the King-Prophet-Musician was made manifest in the 19th century A.D., is frequently referred to in music annals, but generally remains an inadequately understood term. Students of Schumann have been more interested in his immediate literary roots than in searching farther afield for the true history and meaning of the *Davidsbund*. Aside from the vague acceptance of the fact that Schumann's imaginary and real cohorts were those banded together for conflict with the modern Philistines on the battle field of esthetics, little is grasped of the real significance of David's influence in Schumann's peculiar realm of thought and feeling. For his knowledge of David, resulting in an admiration that inflamed the very spirit of his creative life, Schumann must have gone directly to the Biblical record.

For the formation of the *Davidsbund* (see pages 53, 98–99), Schumann found its source and inspiration in I Samuel 22:1–2 (otherwise called the First Book of Kings): "David therefore ... fled (from Saul) to the cave of Odollam ... And all that were in distress and oppressed with debt and under affliction of mind, gathered themselves unto him: and he became their prince, and there were with him about four hundred men." And, in the next chapter, David requested and received divine guidance (Verse 2): "David consulted the Lord, saying: Shall I go (with the band) and smite the Philistines? And the Lord said to David: Go, and thou shalt smite the Philistines." From this original *Davidsbund*, Schumann undoubtedly derived the idea of organizing kindred souls against what he regarded as

Music: Now and Then

forces inimical to spiritual progress in his day, for a conflict as old as humanity, in which David was and remains the prototype.

But, quite aside from the origin of Schumann's League of David, was the revival of David's spirit of fantasy, as expressed in spontaneous improvisation, in Schumann. It is this "spirit of fantasy" which was, and now stands out as the outstanding characteristic, both of David and Schumann. This is unquestionably a deeply "subjective" interpretation. But it is the divine inner fire of the heart and soul of the figure that looms in the clear light of objective distance, as a towering peak on the horizon of time: DAVID: A COLOSSAL MUSICAL MONUMENT!

Introduction

Several years ago a leading educational institution invited me to teach a course in its regular curriculum, entitled: "The Development of Music." After due consideration, I informed its president that, while I was interested in giving a historical series of lectures, the title lacked accuracy and relevancy. I explained that a more revealing title, for my particular approach to the subject, would be "Historical Changes in Music."

While abundant literary evidences exist, from the earliest times, concerning music, the lack of specific data, in the form of musical notation, instruments, etc., has afforded historians ample excuse to treat of the music of antiquity, and especially origins, with the utmost sketchiness and ambiguity. While this is a subject of great interest, what we are specifically concerned with at this particular moment is not material evidences of musical origins and expansion, but the part music played in the lives of the ancients, and the extent of its use, whether utilitarian or esthetic; as well as music in our own time, with similar considerations in mind. For purposes of dramatic juxtaposition, the first shall be last, the last, first.

It is necessary, in developing a proper sense of values, to differentiate between those things which are of the

Music: Now and Then

spirit, justly to be viewed as *timeless*, and those whose relation is to the ephemeral, the passing, or, merely, *timely*. In the contemplation of those musical works that have withstood the vicissitudes of time, surviving from other days, this is not difficult. Indeed, it is self-evident, and need not detain us at this point. What we are concerned with, here and now, both with relation to the past and to the present, is: to what uses has man put one of the noblest gifts of the Almighty? For music, by its nature, and long before the discovery and development of the idea of *ethos* by the ancient Greeks, is, potentially, more universal in function, irrespective of time, place, people, and occasion, than any other of God's gifts to man. I say "potentially" advisedly, with consideration of the nature and manifold purposes of music, which throughout the ages has served man equally in work and play, in peace and war, in joy and sorrow — in life and death.

Now: Music in Our Time

Unfortunately, even the noblest of God's blessings may be and frequently are abused, rather than used for high and intended purpose, in a vaunted "Christian" civilization in which nations, organizations, and individuals futilely strive for material domination and spiritual peace by one and the same means, in an atmosphere of hate and fear; in which unthinking millions, in their frantic attempt to survive present chaos, having neither time nor inclination to acknowledge the Redeemer of mankind, unwittingly do so whenever they vacuously indicate the year on a letter or legal document, of however degraded a nature: the year of the birth of Jesus Christ.

❧ The Music Industry

Music, in America, in the manner of other great enterprises, has been manipulated so that it has become what has been termed a billion-dollar-plus industry. The principal "uses" served by various super-organizations controlling this vast industrialization of the universal expressions of man's spirit are: the concert field, radio, television, records, films, Broadway, opera, symphony

Music: Now and Then

orchestras, schools, and, last but not least in influence, the juke box.

There are, to be sure, other uses made of music, some of which are rapidly dwindling because of the growth of modern invention and the pressure of super-salesmanship, whereby wide dissemination for vast masses tends to crush lesser and relatively unprofitable activities, such as those in the theatre, home, and by amateur groups.

While sounding a pessimistic fanfare, the picture would not be complete without recognition of the fact that the outward, seemingly preponderant manifestations and uses of music, under the pressure of the market, do not tell the whole story. These more obvious considerations, greeting our ears at every turn, are largely whipped up by the winds of publicity. They are primarily whitecaps on the surface of the deeper undercurrents, which, undeterred in their immutable courses, continue their calm, inner movement, unperturbed by the vain howlings of passing winds. The nature of these timeless undercurrents, as well as the more obvious manifestations, are all to be duly considered and evaluated.

The Concert Field

The "concert field" of America is largely dominated by two monopolistic concert agencies in New York, whose antennae extend to the far ends of the country. Their

The Concert Field

control is so complete that artists chosen "for sale" throughout America must have received metropolitan acclaim of such a nature as to justify "Ballyhoo" — their idol and that of the concert-going public. A hero-worshipping public is thus built up, whose anticipation at seeing and hearing their favorites is fanned into a vanity of consuming intensity. A by-product of the monopolistic control of America's concert life is the fantastic weight ascribed to the favorable dicta of New York critics, the *sine qua non* of a concert artist's salability. The demand must be created, whetted by anticipation, and glutted by vanity.

Needless to say, the majority of the millions who comprise the national concert-going public know little or nothing of the music performed, nor are they impelled to become participants in music making, since the commercialized forces in control are always prepared to serve their vast and heterogeneous public, by one means or another, with the ready prepared, pre-digested article. The public is a huge all-consuming mouth, always to be filled — for a price. Musically and spiritually the audiences are largely passive and always on the receiving end.

In the presence of the prevalent state of music, it requires a considerable readjustment to realize that music by its very nature is primarily a social force — not so merely by attendance and lending an ear, but by participation; and by use upon an appropriate occasion. It is difficult for us to realize that the present occasion for musical performance: the appointed time and place of a concert, at a price, is a modern contrivance which

Music: Now and Then

has robbed music making of much of its pristine power. But of this — more anon.

There are other considerations with relation to the circumscribed control of the vast and highly remunerative national concert field, such as the resultant limitations of oft-repeated repertoire, season after season. Such by-products are important details, but the general panorama is what concerns us at this time.

The Radio Antennae

Radio, it has been observed, has been instrumental in creating more listeners than ever before in the history of mankind. While statistics seem to confirm this contention, it may appropriately be remarked that "nothing lies like statistics" and, I may add, especially when they are correct! Degree of attention; capacity for hearing; power of concentration — together with its fruits: contemplation and meditation; and the resulting depths and heights of experience, are all essential concomitant determining factors in the performance of music in ideal circumstances and surroundings. They all have immediate bearing upon the listening experience and our intellectual, emotional, and spiritual reactions. While granting the self-evident, we have been led to the conclusion, not embraced in statistical findings, that, by virtue of radio, never before in the history of the human race did so many people listen to so much so-called music, to their esthetic damnation, and to so

The Radio Antennae

much "good" music, superficially. Even the best music, in innumerable instances, in homes and public places, has become mere background for small talk, games, and carousing. Here, again, the unfortunate by-products in the form of cheap tunes, disgusting words, crooners, "marijuana music" (variously known in popular parlance as "swing," "jive," "boogie-woogie," etc.), are all so familiar that we are in imminent danger of taking them for granted. I shall permit you to develop the idea implicit in this passing observation — the great danger in which contemporary civilization finds itself when there is accepted without effectual protest the pollution of universal air-waves by the cheap, the trivial, the unthinking; by the substitution of motion for emotion in music, for casting the pearls of a great tradition before swine, for the spawning of sound effects and accompanying "music," so-called, by all that is vulgar, vain, and ephemeral.

It was to have been hoped that the desecration of one of the greatest of man's "discoveries" might have created a revulsion of feeling sufficiently powerful to have brought about its reform or destruction. But such salutary result has not taken place nor is it likely to occur. Radio has done its work too well. Insidiously, relentlessly, the ears of the multitudes have become inured, indoctrinated, indifferent, as the case may be. We have reached the point of infamy where even the horror of a singing commercial scarcely affects us.

So, the advent of television and its outrageous music, from the very beginning, causes little surprise and scarcely a protest. I recently remarked to an intellec-

Music: Now and Then

tual friend that the idea of seeing the people one hears by radio was almost more than one could bear. He replied: "It is still worse to hear what one sees!" It would seem to be a reversible, if hopeless, situation. In any event, television has added insult to injury.

Broadway's musical offering, in spite of extravagant claims for its contribution to the contemporary theatre, has been made on the altar of vanity. It represents all that is smart, superficial, ephemeral, and streamlined in the showcase of our "civilization." As, in the case of Hollywood, Broadway feeds the insatiable appetite for the newest, the latest, attracting, *en passant*, some glamorous stars of opera, to be recorded for a short-lived posterity. "Box office" is its final test of value, and success lies in shekels.

◆§ Records

Records, placing in permanent form the most "successful" performances and products of the concert stage, radio, opera, and films, follow, both quantitatively and qualitatively, in their wake. Their influence, for better or worse, becomes more deeply rooted, hence of deeper concern. They may be viewed as an effect, not a cause, since recording moguls keep a weather eye upon the products and by-products of the various associated industries, realizing that "nothing succeeds like success," if seized upon while it is "hot," realizing, for financial reasons, that, in most instances, "today's hit

Hollywood

is tomorrow's embarrassment." So the ephemeral, in a huge preponderance of cases, is cast in "permanent" form — to be rapidly withdrawn from the market when the latest musical fad pushes it aside, but not soon enough!

❦ Hollywood

The hopes held by many for music in the films, including some of our leading creative musicians, have been shattered in much the same way as in radio. While many performing musicians, and particularly vocal "coaches," have taken up residence in the world's movie center and reaped a golden harvest, Hollywood has proven the land of frustration to composers. Its influence upon a most important aspect of our musical life has been in inverse ratio to its potentialities. The creative musician has become a mere adjunct to movie production, turning out, mainly, background music, sound effects or special songs for "stars of the screen." Many a composer of talent has gone to Hollywood with great expectations and left in disillusionment, with heavy heart — if heavier purse. Those who have remained in this artificial, esthetically false, tinsel heaven have sacrificed what musical ideals and integrity they may have had when they went there. At best, the musical output of Hollywood has been as pretentious as it has been inept; at its worst, it has pandered to slushy sentimentality, expensive cheapness, and the vulgarity of the times. The performing "artists" who have been spawned and become "stars of the screen" are unworthy of serious consideration. Hollywood, that Mecca of the world's crooners, is a blot upon the musical life of America, in spite of the fact that occasionally artists of distinction temporarily succumb to its golden lure.

And the harm done a vast public, whose favorite form of relaxation is attendance at the movies, is incalculable. Music has and will survive, as have others of God's misused gifts to mankind; but people have only one life, of short duration, to live on earth. That life, all too frequently contaminated by such degradations, should be the object of our profound concern and action.

⋅§ Opera

Opera, our most expensive and fashionable musical manifestation, is the brilliant jewel in the musical crown of our vanity. Dominated by the Metropolitan Opera of New York, which, by radio and brief, limited tours, reaches the outlying parts of the country, opera in America has never taken deep root nor shown signs of becoming an indigenous growth. Measured in terms of its fashionableness, it attains the heights of "success," as we know it. On the other hand, evaluated by its lack of creative life, its false claims to preëminence, it may well, one day, be recognized as belonging in a category we so delight in imputing to past eras that meet with disapproval, i.e. that of decadence. And, to speak in terms well known to all, its monopolistic practices might well come under the governmental provisions of a corrupt practices act. This is true, in spite of the fact that we have "wandering minstrels" in traveling operatic troupes, not unrelated to "things of shreds and patches," who eke out some sort of musical and material existence in transcontinental tours.

❧ Orchestral Music

America possesses more, larger, and better orchestras than any other country or time, directed, for the greater part, by eminent foreign-born and foreign-trained conductors. That these conductors are relatively superior to our scarce, home-grown variety, is incontestable. The reasons for this are not difficult to discover. Ever since the days of P. T. Barnum, and before, we have delighted in attracting the great in the field of art from other lands, by offering them financial rewards unheard of in their countries. The precedent for this is akin to the acquisition of Greek music and musicians by the Romans when they were on the ascent as a dominant power, and had neither the time nor the patience to develop a musical culture of their own, when it could be purchased, ready-made, elsewhere. In addition, we have enjoyed the supreme vanity of basking in the reflected glory of the high-priced, great of music, that we alone have been able to lure and maintain.

Music: Now and Then

The commercialized control of our musical industry has done everything in its power to perpetuate these conditions, making little provision for our musical future; satisfied to reap a golden harvest from the imported, glamorous great. The managers, particularly of orchestras, have thereby hampered the development of our own and the education of the public to receive our own, on the same basis as we welcome those from afar.

In spite of a few conductors who encourage the contemporary creative musician, the symphonic repertoire, with squirrel-in-the-cage reiteration, largely revolves around the oft repeated, the "successful," the *passively accepted*, the latter consideration being that with which we are immediately concerned in this discussion. The public has expanded, but it is largely apathetic and not at all concerned with creative aspects of music nor with *participation*. Tribute to the proven great in music, both in compositions, conductors, and performers, is a form of vanity that has attained new distinction in our civilization. A growingly apathetic public welcomes refuge in safely acclaiming the accepted, without questioning or ability to question. Thus we see the return of a period of virtuosity referred to contemptuously by the musicologist, Nef, as one in which "The public made obeisance to a superficial claptrap." Only our tribute is typically different from that of the past: being on a bigger, if not better, scale.

Music Education

The most important factor, potentially, in our picture, is music education. How is it meeting its colossal responsibility — the challenge of duty to a vastly expanded public?

The status of professional schools is important, in the training of professionals for public performance, whether as soloists or in ensembles; the formation of creative musicians and the preparation of those who are to be instrumental in teaching the millions of young in our schools, public and parochial. It goes without saying, that the last consideration is, by far, the most important. For without the proper training of the many, the relatively few — creators and performers — will have no fertile soil for growth and expansion. The weaknesses in our musical structure may only be corrected at educational roots; hence the responsibility devolving upon those who are to guide the young. Little hope may be safely entertained for correcting the malformations of the adult musical mind.

One of the most striking weaknesses of the music schools responsible for training young professionals is that they are primarily located in the section of the United States along the seaboard, from Boston to Philadelphia. Heavily endowed institutions in a limited area attract aspirants — largely for fame — from the entire country, even the world. They are primarily eager for musical honors which will prepare them for glamorous careers: on the concert stage, in radio, opera, films, etc. These schools have turned out and are still

Music: Now and Then

graduating young performers most of whom are doomed to frustration in the overcrowded metropolitan market.

And how often have we witnessed the procedure existing in our professional schools: the student emerges from the classroom at the appointed time, fantastically termed "commencement," suddenly to be cast upon society — to sink or swim! The student, now become "professional," is confronted by a reality that he is inadequately prepared to face: often "all dressed up and nowhere to go." The result is a world in which there are far too many disillusioned and frustrated musicians who discover, too late, that their wares are a glut upon a market tragically limited by false and superficial values. This latter consideration has also to do with weaknesses inherent in our general educational structure.

Students of greatest talent, i.e. those with creative ability, have even less opportunity than performers. As a social, economically secure entity, the composer is non-existent. Several years ago I did research for the Rockefeller Foundation in the field of the economic status of the creative musician in America. As a result of tabulating the mass of confidential information furnished by the professional composers, including highly paid hacks in Hollywood, it was revealed that slightly more than five percent of the incomes of our composers is derived from creative work, whether in commissions, royalties, awards, or performance fees.

Since the public has come to believe that the performer is the beginning and end of all music, the greater attraction is toward public careers, in emulation of

Music Education

those for whom financial rewards have been great. This has left, for final consideration, both here and in education, those who are destined for the training of the young — in whom our greatest hopes lie.

For several years I happened to be associated with one of the leading professional music schools, in which I served on the jury which placed entrants in their respective categories for inculcation into the requirements of the various branches of the musical profession. Those aspirants who manifested the greatest background and possibilities, as performers, were enrolled with eminent teachers for intensive study for the concert stage. Those whose outlook for success in the field of virtuosity was doubtful were entered in pedagogy classes, to be trained as private teachers. Those showing the least capacity were placed in "public school music courses." The latter groups, with no hope of future brilliant careers, were relegated to the hum-drum in a school which endeavored to attract the most ambitious, spectacular students. Yet it may easily be comprehended, even by the least experienced, that the training, not to mention the innate qualifications as well as background, of those to be entrusted with education of the young is of the utmost importance. This generally prevailing attitude toward the teaching of music to children in our schools has primarily been responsible for its ineptitude. To be sure, that teaching has expanded enormously, but the statistics, in the manner of all such polls or compilations, reveal not the imponderable things of true values, but the quantitative matters which appeal to the eye, if not the reason.

Music: Now and Then

◆§ The Juke Box

Our time has witnessed waves of reform, not always equalled by their equivalent in virtue, that have publicly condemned, seized, and possibly destroyed everything that smacks of gambling, chance, getting-something-for-little, even to the pin-ball machine. This latter, relatively innocent purveyor of a-little-amusement-at-little-cost, had come under the ban because of its control by racketeers, with the attendant evils and crimes. Yet, the most pernicious of contemporary infernal machines — the juke box — has been permitted to remain, polluting the atmosphere of public places frequented by a vast public in search of inexpensive recreation. The juke box unashamedly dispenses horrible musical concoctions of, by, and for morons, to the preserving and increasing of their moral and spiritual vacuity. It thrives best where alcoholic drinks add their final touch to the dulling of the intellect, with the sublimation of all true thought, and the stimulation of sensuality. If the moral sense of the reformers who have done away with pin-ball machines were as keen as their power to detect the evils of gangsterism, the juke box would have been the first to come under the ban.

◆§ Contemporary Music

Finally, in this rapidly moving survey of musical activities in our time, we have to consider the nature of

Contemporary Music

that music which is created today, whether it be what is termed, variously, high-brow or "classical," or, on the other hand, "popular" music. Nor would the picture be complete without some recognition of the fact that musical undercurrents, undeterred by the passing fury of outward manifestations, have existed and will continue to function when the reverberations of the present are scarcely heard or recollected.

So-called "classical" music, a much abused and misused term, we shall consider, for the purposes of this discussion, as music written by professionally trained composers for serious consideration, whether in the concert hall or elsewhere. It has to do with what is known as "art" forms. As founder and director of the Composers' Forum, which since 1935 has publicly presented a cross-section of the contemporary output of creative musicians in America, I have had unique opportunity to come in intimate contact with this music.

It is well to remember that the music of any period in our history remains, after the event, one of the most revealing evidences of the character of a particular time. Hence it is possible for the informed listener to determine, with a reasonable degree of accuracy or approximation, the period from which a work derives, even in the case of unfamiliar music. This is possible not only from the form of a composition but from its style, mirrored inexorably from the spirit of the time and place from which it emerged. Such influences make a wider and more indelible stamp upon the musical physiognomy of music than the individual characteristics of the composers themselves, no matter how important they may be. In other words, whether or not it is apparent during the particular time in which a work appears, in retrospect, in the revealing light of historical perspective, the interdependent form and substance of music are seen to be molded in the spiritual image of their own time. Let us understand that this rather sweeping generalization must be qualified as applying to those works of any period which are sufficiently timeless in spiritual essence, as well as more obvious but interrelated features, to withstand the vicissitudes of time and eventually emerge with universality of appeal and meaning. History is, in large part, a process of elimination, and much that seems representative and important when new disappears when seen from the vantage point of distance, in which the merely timely vanishes, and the timeless looms high on the horizon. The stature of music is eventually gauged, therefore, by its towering peaks rather than by the foothills that surely led up to them or by the host of imitators who unthinkingly followed, not realizing that the summit had been reached and that they were merely descending into an abyss of inconsequence and oblivion.

From the lessons we have learned from the past, it easily might be concluded that judgments of the musical present should be left to the future, at which time they will be taken care of properly and automatically. While not claiming the "long-distance view" that graces so many myopic but omniscient self-appointed observers of the present, we can contemplate our time fear-

Contemporary Music

lessly and fairly, even without fore-knowledge of what the inevitable historical process may eventually eliminate.

Within our own time we have witnessed an important upsurge in creative musical activity, especially here in America. This is due to several causes, not the least of which has been the centering of power, mainly material, in America, following the bankruptcy of other countries as a result of war. The material power was unquestionably ours; the challenge to our spiritual and intellectual resources equally great. With increased opportunities at home for study and stimulation to the young creative minds, we have had not only a vast increase in the number of creative musicians, but a commensurate expansion in the use of the materials of their craft.

We remarked earlier that "the music of any period in our history remains one of the most revealing evidences of the character of a particular time." I might amplify this statement with the observation that even when the material power of a given period has been relegated to the limbo of the past, music which, as it were, distills the very essence of its time and preserves it for posterity, either in tradition, writing, or both, remains the inexorable, immutable testimony of the spirit of a time and people.

It is not necessary to expound our great strength, our vast might, centered in improved atomic bombs, B-47s (already outmoded, "they say"), etc., which back up our struggles in the cold war to preserve the imbalance of power in the struggle for peace. These

Music: Now and Then

things are screamed from daily headlines and in the halls of statesmen. What concerns us is: has music, in the manner of the historical function claimed by us, kept pace with these all-too-familiar developments? The inevitable answer is in the affirmative!

Indeed, the "expansion in the use of the materials of their craft," as in the field of science and the realm of all intellectual pursuits, has reached a new high in the annals of mankind. At the same time, spirituality is considered as something naïve, outmoded. As a result, we have much music of vast physical proportions, an amazing complexity of polyrhythms, polytonality, and "what have you," with little inner meaning or communicative power.

But, at the same time, our creative musicians have substituted master-craftsmanship for the true creative processes, which might well be learned from the working procedures of many "inspired" composers of the past, such as Mozart, Haydn, Schubert, Beethoven, *et al.* In failing this consideration, they have taken the part to be greater than the whole, and have in fact ignored the chief quickening, even if imponderable, element: the life-giving spirit. As well might a scientist, having assembled all the known and proven component parts of an organism, claim that he had created a living, functioning thing. So the musical embryo, minus the quickening spirit, is now termed a musical creation!

Composers, in attaining new technical freedom and complexity, have sold their spiritual birthright for means leading to a dead-end. With many the formula is, frequently: "The more platitudinous, the louder."

Contemporary Music

How often, in listening to a new work by one of today's great, have I recalled the story of the English rector who, having suddenly taken ill, asked his curate to read the sermon he had written for the Sunday service. The rector had made marginal notations for the sermon's delivery. The curate, busily reading the unfamiliar text as well as the marginal directions, was doing his best to give life to the script, when he was astonished to see an underscored notation: "*This is a weak spot, yell like hell!*" Well might many contemporary composers be as frank!

The historical process of elimination is rapidly taking care of many of such works, but the written record will remain to remind us and the future of the time when the bodies of some prehistoric creatures vanished because their physical proportions exceeded any other excuse for being.

That such tonal excesses should rapidly bring about a revulsion of feeling, was inevitable. So we witness our best craftsmen turning in desperation to neo-classicism, neo-romanticism, aping technical procedures of the recent as well as the more remote past. I say "technical procedures" advisedly, as they have failed to revive the inner spirit which alone gave the originals of these various styles their timelessness and universality. Revulsion and the constraints of necessity have turned contemporary composers to a re-evaluation of the past, completely reversing their recent antipathy for their valid musical progenitors. But, unable to invoke the spirit of these past eras emanating from "inspiration," their empty and futile attempts succeed only in musical post-mortems which have granted life neither to the present nor the past. What has been produced has mainly been a fantastically emasculated version of forms that seem strangely outmoded in the hands of contemporary composers. Their principal claim to "genius" is that stroke by which they attempt to rationalize the lack of what, not possessing it, they deny and anathematize.

"Popular" Music

"Popular" music, both in production and dissemination, has also entered a new phase, characteristic of our time. In the presence of commercialization, the idea of folk music, music growing indigenously from a people, from its very roots, is as outmoded as "inspiration" to a serious composer of today. In place of true, simple, direct folk expression, we have the latest "hit" spawned under the demands of a market with antennae extending through every means of communication and distribution. This music, like water, does not tend to rise above its source. The source is to be traced to the lowest instincts of mankind, representing the debasement of God-given attributes. Their contamination has led to an esthetic hell that has brought "popular" music into a state of damnation without similar extent in the history of mankind. It may seem that undue emphasis is placed here upon something that is so ephemeral and valueless. Unfortunately, this music is not merely an effect, a bad odor arising from the cesspool of civiliza-

"Popular" Music

tion. Its evil spirit is the direct cause of the mental and spiritual contamination of millions, whom the commercialized musical interests are organized to exploit for material gain, at no matter what moral cost and infamy. That we have become accustomed to such things to the degree that we pass them by, heedlessly, even if we do not accept and embrace them, is one of the most tragic commentaries of the age. Nothing is more fatal to thought and thinking, to growth, than to become so habituated to daily contacts, whether tangible or intangible, that we no longer react to them. To ignore is to invite ignorance!

Musical Undercurrents

In the foregoing panorama, we have witnessed the predominant aspects of music of this era, music controlled by the market, for the majority of mankind.

Unseen, unheeded, unheard by millions, the deeper undercurrents of music, indivisible from spiritual experience, pursue their immutable course, to the glory of God and the elevation of mankind. Mass is still sung in churches with good intention, if not always, because of human frailty, with undimmed realization. But how vital this intention in a world degraded by evil! The preservation of music at the altar of God is the rainbow of promise that all is not lost, and that a brighter day dawns for humanity in the realm of the spirit, when all men will realize the glory of God in music.

Then: Our Musical Heritage from the Bible

«If I speak with the tongues of men and of angels, and have not charity, I am become as sounding brass, or a tinkling cymbal.»

(St. Paul to the Corinthians.) (I Cor. 13: 1)

Having referred, in passing, to "our musical heritage," let us turn our eyes and ears toward those earlier times when men, generally, seemed to be more aware of God's presence, even if, in their self-conferred strength, they sometimes failed to live up to His promises.

One of the most intriguing aspects of Biblical history is that many of God's gifts have not been recorded until they were developed to a high degree of usefulness to man. This is particularly true of music. While no musical notation is extant from Biblical times, there is ample evidence of the following: that, by the sixth generation from Cain, music was already in practice; that it had become, or became at this point, a family tradition with nomadic people (Gen. 4:21); that instruments for its performance were in existence and used by Cain's descendants: "And his brother's (Jabel's) name was Jubal; he was the father of them that play upon the harp and the organs." This unquestionably refers to both stringed and wind instruments. You may recall that the great composer Handel made a musical setting to a text, "O, had I Jubal's lyre." Handel's intentions were probably good, although his choice of the "lyre," a later Greek instrument, may scarcely be condoned in the name of poetic license.

Music: Now and Then

Edgar Allan Poe was on much safer ground in using a non-Biblical name in his similarly inspired, ecstatic:

> "In heav'n a spirit doth dwell,
> Whose heart strings are a lute.
> None sing so wildly well,
> As the angel, Israfel,
> And the giddy stars,
> So legends tell,
> Ceasing their hymns,
> Attend the spell of his voice,
> All mute."

◆§ Concerning Points of Inquiry

From the point of the earliest mention of music as a *fait accompli*, as an established tradition, we shall proceed with an inquiry into the various uses made of music from the seventh generation after Adam through the beginnings of the Christian era. Since men were what they were, and still are, *use* presupposes *abuse**; and we shall also turn our attention to occasions when God's gift of music was misused; even withdrawn completely from His bounty.

Since means of making music was an important factor with our antecedents, as it is today, it is also of interest to note the nature and number of instruments used, in addition to that most natural mode of musical expression, the human voice; the organization both of

---

* For the benefit of those likely to view this statement philosophically or dogmatically, the reference is purely *de facto*, i.e. historical.

A Biblical Preface

music and musicians in insuring its and their preservation in the service of God and man; and, above all, the physical and spiritual power of music in man's struggles, of both the body and spirit. For let us remember that music in Biblical times was not considered an art, a thing of vanity and enjoyment in times of leisure, practiced by seekers of fame and fortune. It was clearly instituted for the preservation of man and the glory of God, and in this dual service its potentialities were realized and cherished.

A Biblical Preface

In supporting this thesis, I have had recourse to the Biblical record, and as preliminary to the particularization which justly must proceed from generalization, I shall quote a most appropriate foreword, from Second Machabees, second chapter: "For considering ... the multitude of the matter, we have taken care for those indeed that are willing to read, that it might be a pleasure of mind: and for the studious, that they may more easily commit to memory: and that all that read might receive profit. And as to ourselves indeed, in undertaking this work of abridging, we have taken in hand no easy task, yea rather a business full of watching and sweat. But as they that prepare a feast, and seek to satisfy the will of others: for the sake of many, we willingly undergo the labor, leaving to the authors the exacting handling of every particular, and as for ourselves, according to the plan proposed; ... to collect all that is to be known, to put the discourse in order, and curiously to discuss every particular point, is the duty of the author of a history: But to pursue brevity of speech is to be granted to him that maketh an abridgment.... Let this be enough by way of a preface ... "

◆§ Use of Single Instruments

Inasmuch as the age of virtuosity *per se* was not in flower in Biblical times, even the use of single instruments presupposes a worthy occasion. However, we are not to infer that musical skills in performance were neglected, as we shall see. Performers were prepared to serve where and when the occasion arose, but that occasion was not mere display for the delectation of onlookers.

Probably the earliest record of the therapeutic use of music was that of David playing on the harp for King Saul (I Kings 16). The servants of Saul said: "Let our lord give orders, and thy servants ... will seek out *a man skilful in playing on the harp,* that when the evil spirit of the Lord is upon thee, he may play with his hand, and thou mayest bear it more easily." And Saul replied: "Provide me then *some man that can play well,* and bring him to me." So David, "*a skilful player ... took his harp, and played* with his hand, and *Saul was refreshed, and was better.*"

Use of Single Instruments

In the foregoing instance, as in those to follow, curiosity as to what David played, how it must have sounded on a primitive instrument of which Hector Berlioz remarked sardonically, many hundreds of years later, that "a harpist is one who spends half of his life tuning his harp, and the other half playing out of tune," must go unsatisfied. This, along with our desire to know something of Saul's likes and dislikes, or taste, as well as knowledge of music, along with a multiplicity of other interesting points, must remain unrevealed, although a fertile field for the imagination.

Later, at the anointing of Solomon as King, we read (III Kings 1:40) that "*the people played with pipes, and rejoiced with great joy.*" The "pipes" were unquestionably the precursors of our woodwinds, and, by many Biblical accounts, were in common use for many hundreds of years before Christ. In fact the Lord (according to St. Luke 7:31-32) said: "Whereunto then shall I liken the men of this generation? . . . They are like children sitting in the market place . . . and saying: *We have piped to you, and you have not danced:* we have mourned, and you have not wept." So we find that the joyful wind instruments were commonly used for rejoicing and dancing from the earliest times, without combination with other instruments, on secular occasions. That pipes, to be thought of as instruments resembling the flute, were in use "from the earliest times" is further attested by the words of the Lord to Ezechiel (Ezech. 28:13): "*Thy pipes were prepared in the day that thou wast created;*" which would indicate the beginning of time.

Music: Now and Then

St. Augustine unmistakably showed his deep veneration for musical instruments and their importance in bringing God's gifts to man, when he spoke of "that *psaltery of ten strings:* Thy ten commandments." The metaphorical allusion to music in such a connection shows how deeply the idea of its use in God's service was infused in the spirit of the great Saint.

Incidentally, we may add the "psalter" to our growing list of ancient stringed instruments, as opposed to those which were sounded by wind, or blowing, such as the "organs" and "pipes" which we have already encountered.

The SOUND OF THE TRUMPET

"Yet ever and anon a trumpet sounds from the hid battlements of Eternity."

Of all the instruments of antiquity that were used on diverse occasions, with the greatest potentialities for both God and man, the *trumpet* was unique. Unlike the instruments already mentioned, being made of metal (see Num. 10:1) and controlled by breath, it probably had greater dynamic range and carrying power than any other instrument. It could be heard by vast multitudes, whether engaged in the worship of God or going into battle, whether soaring into the Mount or sounding the alarm. The diversity of occasions for appropriate use of the trumpet, both for spiritual and physical results, was practically unlimited.

The Sound of the Trumpet

When God spoke to Moses (Exod. 19:13), saying: "When *the trumpet shall begin to sound,* then let them (the Israelites) go up into the Mount," the utilization of the trumpet, for the purpose of calling the people to worship, must already have been well established. For the reactions to God's command, both in hearers and those who sounded the trumpet, were such that previous experience may safely be assumed (Exod. 19:16): "*And the noise of the trumpet sounded exceeding loud, and the people that was in the camp, feared.*" "And," with the earliest record of musical dynamics and augmentation, "*the sound of the trumpet grew by degrees louder and louder, and was drawn out to a greater length:* Moses spoke, and God answered him." (Exod. 19:19)

One must keep in mind, after all, that the Bible is not a history of music! As we observed earlier, even the first mention of music and musical instruments did not occur until they were well established and developed. There was no intention or attempt to trace the step-by-step changes, from inception to growth into practical means and instituted procedures. So we come upon the various well developed stages of music, in the course of searching the Scriptures, with frequent astonishment and wonder. The force of revelation, which greets us at every turn, in no wise detracts from our comprehension and search for knowledge. On the contrary, it inflames us with something of that spirit which must have illumined our forebears in the use of music for their own preservation and the realization of God's intentions.

The establishment of music, in fulfilling the will of

Music: Now and Then

God, was so clearly ordered and carefully organized, that it furnishes irrefutable evidence of the divine institution of a musical tradition, not only for the worship and glory of the Almighty, but for use in war, for banquets and festival days, for holocausts and remembrance. (Num. 10:1–10): "And the Lord spoke to Moses, saying: Make thee two *trumpets of beaten silver*, that thou mayest call together the multitude ... And when thou shalt *sound the trumpets*, all the multitude shall gather unto thee to the door of the tabernacle of the covenant. *If thou sound but once*, the princes and heads of the multitude of Israel shall come to thee. But *if the sound of the trumpets be longer*, and *with interruption*, they that are on the east side, shall first go forward. And *at the second sounding and like noise of the trumpet*, they on the south side ... And after this manner shall the rest do, when *the trumpets shall sound for a march ... the sound of the trumpets shall be plain, and they shall not make a broken sound. And the sons of Aaron the priest shall sound the trumpets: and this shall be an ordinance forever in your generations. If you go forth to war ... you shall sound aloud with the trumpets, and there shall be a remembrance of you before the Lord your God*, that you may be delivered out of the hands of your enemies. *If at any time you shall have a banquet and on your festival days, and on the first days of your months, you shall sound the trumpets over the holocausts, and the sacrifices of peace offerings, that they may be to you for a remembrance of your God.*" Injunction for the liturgical use of music is again emphasized (Num. 29:1): "The first day also of the

The Sound of the Trumpet

seventh month shall be venerable and holy unto you; you shall do no servile work therein, because *it is the day of the sounding and of trumpets.*"

These extraordinarily complete commands of the Lord not only instituted the ordinance, but explicitly indicated the material for and manner of making the instruments, the deploying and timing of participants, and specific instructions for performance. Their detailed and comprehensive nature leaves no doubt as to the great importance intended for music in the lives of God's creatures. Nothing was left to chance or caprice. Music was clearly ordained as a part of the Almighty's endless bounty to mankind.

The careful organization of music for the pursuits of peace and the worship of God, also served man in time of conflict. The shift from peacetime negligence to wartime economy and organization was not such a problem in those days, nor did it, apparently, afflict mankind to the same extent in Biblical times as it has in more recent crises. Thus it scarcely surprises when, later, before the walls of Jericho, God commanded Josue (Josue 6): "Go round about the city, all ye fighting men, once a day: so shall ye do for six days. And on the seventh day *the priests shall take the seven trumpets, which are used in the jubilee,* and shall go before the ark of the covenant: and you shall go about the city seven times: and *the priests shall sound the trumpets.* And *when the voice of the trumpet shall give a longer and broken tune, and shall sound in your ears,* all the people shall shout together with a very great shout, and the walls of the city shall fall to the ground."

Music: Now and Then

Josue did as bidden: "And seven of them (the priests), *seven trumpets, which are used in the jubilee* ... went before the ark of the Lord walking and *sounding the trumpets* ... And when in the seventh going about *the priests sounded with the trumpets,* Josue said to all Israel: Shout: for the Lord hath delivered the city to you ... So all the people making a shout, and *the trumpets sounding,* when *the voice and the sound thundered in the ears of the multitude,* the walls forthwith fell down." It is quite apparent that tonal excesses were not a commonplace at the time of Josue!

The vital part played by the trumpet in mobilizing and directing the Israelites for conflict with various enemies is recorded on numerous occasions. There is ample evidence that, in the mind and soul of the people, the trumpet imaged God's voice and word. So, "*the spirit of the Lord came upon Gedeon, and he sounded the trumpet* and called together (the people) to follow him." (Judges 6:34). Again, Gedeon speaking to the Israelites (Judges 7:18-22): "When the trumpet shall sound in my hand, do you also *blow the trumpets* on every side of the camp ... they held their lamps in their left hands, and with their right hands *the trumpets which they blew* ... And *the three hundred men ... persisted sounding the trumpets.*"

Battle signals of diverse kinds were in common use. Their code is not recorded, but the mere fact that they were understood and obeyed without confusion, under stress, indicates the existence of such a code, in which the people were well versed. Hence, we read (II Kings 2:28): "Then Joab *sounded the trumpet, and all the*

The Sound of the Trumpet

army stood still." The extremes, from action to repose, were indubitably covered by organized and clearly differentiated signals, precluding all possibility of misunderstanding by the multitude.

As the code embraced signals for deploying and entering into battle, so it provided for refraining from pursuit (II Kings 18:16): "And Joab *sounded the trumpet, and kept the people from pursuing* after Israel in their flight."

Throughout the ages, response to the "sound of the trumpet" was so assured, that hundreds of years later St. Paul (I Cor. 14:8) could only envision hypothetical failure of battle signals to defection on the part of the trumpeter himself: "For if the *trumpet* give an uncertain sound, who shall prepare himself to the battle?"

Later, at the time of the rebuilding of the walls of Jerusalem, Nehemias commanded (II Esd. 4:20): "In what place soever you shall hear *the sound of the trumpet, run all thither* unto us: our God will fight for us."

Job alone admits of circumstances in which *the sound of the trumpet* might be disregarded, when he graphically portrays the power and providence of God (Job 39:24–25): "neither doth he make account when *the noise of the trumpet soundeth.* When *he heareth the trumpet* he saith: Ha, ha: he smelleth the battle afar off . . ."

No wonder that Jeremias cried out (Jer. 4:21): "How long shall I see men fleeing away, how long shall I hear *the sound of the trumpet?*" and that God, rejecting the hypocrisies of the Jews (Isa. 58:1), abjured: "Cry, cease not, *lift up thy voice like a trumpet,*

Music: Now and Then

and shew my people their wicked doings, and the house of Jacob their sins."

The final desolation of Israel is fearsomely prophesied by Ezechiel (Ezech. 7:14) as a time in which the sounding of the trumpet will no longer summon the people to battle and victory: "*Blow the trumpet*, let all be made ready, yet there is none to go to the battle: for my (God's) wrath shall be upon all the people thereof." The prophet could envisage no greater depth of despair than a world in which the power of the trumpet's sounding, as of God's voice, no longer rouses mankind to action. As Amos cried (Amos 3:6): "Shall *the trumpet sound in a city, and the people not be afraid?*"

The dire tragedy of failure to respond to the trumpet's sound is further prophesied by Ezechiel, in the words of God, saying (Ezech. 33:2–4): "When I ... make him (a man) watchman (over the people) and he sees the sword coming upon the land, and *sound the trumpet* ... and he that heareth *the sound of the trumpet*, whosoever he be, and doth not look to himself ... his blood shall be upon his own head." And a warning follows, in case the watchman fails to sound!

The trumpet, as the symbol of doom, in the mouths of the latter-day prophets, prior to the coming of Christ, became as eloquent a word as it had previously been a powerful weapon with the Israelites. At that time the trumpet was still used in urging on to battle, as is recorded in the accounts of Judas Machabeus' defense of the Israelites against those who would have destroyed them (I Mach. 3:53–54): "How shall we be able to stand before their face, unless thou, O God,

The Sound of the Trumpet

help us? Then they *sounded with trumpets,* and cried out with a loud voice." This was no longer the voice of those confident of victory, but the cry of a desperate people, for regeneration. But God heard the entreaties of Judas Machabeus for the preservation of the temple. "They went out of the camp to battle, and they that were with Judas *sounded the trumpet* . . . and the Gentiles were routed . . . " (I Mach. 4:13–14)

Later, Judas Machabeus, still leading the Israelites, when "the cry of the battle went up to heaven *like a trumpet,* . . . said: Fight ye today for your brethren . . . and they *sounded their trumpets,* and cried out in prayer. And the host of Timotheus understood that it was Machabeus, and they fled away before his face." (I Mach. 5:31–33) But the conflict with the armies from Greece continued; they made themselves ready for battle and they *"sounded . . . with trumpets to stir up the army,* and to hasten them forward." (I Mach.6:33, 38)

The embattled Israelites continued their wars of defense and, in 162 B.C., when Judas Machabeus prayed to the Lord (I Mach. 7): "Even so destroy this army in our sight today . . . and the army of Nicanor was defeated and he was slain," and his followers fled, the Israelites pursued after the enemy "and *they sounded the trumpets* after them with signals." And it was recounted that "the land of Juda was quiet for a short time." But it was for a short time only, and the valiant defender of the Israelites, in their last days as a fighting people, before Christ's coming, continued to *"sound the trumpets"* in battle (I Mach. 9:12) up to the very time that he was slain.

Music: Now and Then

Although, as we have seen, the sounding of the trumpet played an important part in battle, and was often the signal for victory, it was not because of any power inherent in the instrument itself nor in its sound, that it served the Israelites. When the trumpet was similarly sounded by those whose battles were not for the divine purposes of the Almighty, it was completely ineffective. Thus we read (II Mach. 15:25, 27) of Nicanor, just prior to his defeat at the hands of Judas Machabeus and the Israelites: "Nicanor, and they that were with him came forward, *with trumpets and songs* ... But Judas (and those that were with him) fighting with their hands but praying to the Lord with their hearts" were led to victory. The source of the music, the purpose of its use, determined its effectiveness. And it was recorded that Nicanor, just prior to his downfall (II Mach. 15:6–7): "being puffed up with exceeding great pride, thought to set up a public monument of victory over Judas. But Machabeus ever trusted with all hope that God would help them." With one, the *sound of the trumpet* aided in achieving victory; with the other, it became a futile sound, even when reinforced by singing!

The predominance of the trumpet in battle tends to obscure its use at other and more peaceful times. Yet even "David," whose predilection was for the harp and singing, "and all the house of Israel brought the ark of the covenant of the Lord with joyful shouting, and *with sound of trumpet*." (II Kings 6:15) And at the anointing of Solomon as king (III Kings 1:39): "they sounded the trumpets" (I Par. 15:24). The references

The Sound of the Trumpet

to the use of the trumpets by priests in the worship of God and on other occasions do not occur as frequently as the allusions to singing and combinations of instruments, as we shall see. However, as we observed before, the intermediate steps, from inception to general use and organization, are not traced in records which do not purport to be a historical survey of music. Fortunately, we are blessed with imagination as well as reason, and are at liberty to reconstruct the missing steps in the musical march, if that were necessary. That the priests did frequently have recourse to the sound of the trumpet, is amply attested, and we may safely assume that the priests were those who were well trained in its use and were called upon as a matter of course, in the regular performance of their duties, to sound the trumpet on many and diverse occasions, even as at the time of the fall of Jericho.

So when (about 914 B.C.) Abia, King of Juda, went to battle against Jeroboam, he said: "Therefore God is the leader of our army, and his *priests who sound with trumpets*, and resound against you ... And they cried to the Lord: and *the priests began to sound with the trumpets* ... and God terrified Jeroboam." (II Par. 13:12–15)

As the trumpet had been a mainstay of the leaders of the Israelites, both in war and in peace, it became the symbol of warning, alarm, and doom, with the prophets, as well as the prophetic voice of the gospel for the conversion of the Jews. In this latter connection Isaias (27:13) prophesied: "And it shall come to pass, that in that day *a noise* shall be made *with a*

Music: Now and Then

great trumpet, and they that were lost... shall adore the Lord in the holy mount in Jerusalem."

The fall of Babylon, in the direful prediction of Jeremias, indeed resounded like the crack of doom in the words (Jer. 51:27): "*sound with the trumpet* among the nations: prepare the nations against her."

The note of forewarning, in poetic imagery, was loudly and graphically sounded by Osee to the Israelites, when God threatened them with destruction for their impiety and idolatry (Osee 8:1): "Let there be *a trumpet in thy throat* like an eagle upon the house of the Lord: because they have transgressed my covenant, and have violated my law." And Joel warned the people of the day of judgment with an outcry (Joel 2:1): "*Blow ye the trumpet* in Sion, *sound an alarm* in my holy mountain, let all the inhabitants of the land tremble: because the day of the Lord cometh, because it is nigh at hand." Abjuring the people to repent, Joel continued (15): "*Blow the trumpet* in Sion, sanctify a fast, call a solemn assembly."

The doom of Moab, foretold by Amos (Amos 2:2) also invoked the fearsome prediction: "Moab shall die with a noise, with *the sound of the trumpet*." The judgment to be visited upon the Kingdom of Juda was even more direful, in Sophonias' warning (Soph. 1:14, 16): "The great day of the Lord is near... and exceeding swift: the voice of the day of the Lord is bitter... That *day is the day of wrath... a day of the trumpet and alarm*..."

The idea of the trumpet as an instrument of alarm and the forewarning of approaching doom was symbol-

The Sound of the Trumpet

ized on many occasions, but nowhere, in the annals of the Old Testament, more eloquently than in the words of the author of First Machabees (I Mach. 4:38-40) in recounting the desolation of Judas Machabeus and the Israelites, when they came upon the profanation of the temple: "And (when) they saw the sanctuary desolate, and the altar profaned . . . they fell down to the ground on their faces, and they *sounded with the trumpets of alarm*, and they cried towards heaven."

After the many centuries in which the trumpet played a vital part in the lives of God's people — in worship and praise, in strivings, struggles and stress, in victory as well as prophecy — there is no cause for wonder that the instrument that had through the ages been symbolic of God's voice, should appear in the mystical revelations to St. John. The trumpet that had been worthy of summoning the chosen people into the mount to hear the voice of the Almighty, naturally sounded in the infinity of His spirit, as it had in terrestrial spaces.

(Apocalypse 1:10): "I was in the spirit on the Lord's day, and heard behind me *a great voice, as of a trumpet* . . . (12) And I turned to see the voice . . . and I saw seven golden candlesticks . . . one like to the Son of man." (Apoc. 4:1) " . . . and behold a door was opened in heaven, and the first *voice* which I heard, as it were, *of a trumpet* speaking with me." (Apoc. 8:2) "And I saw seven angels standing in the presence of God; and *there were given to them seven trumpets.* (6) And the seven angels, who had *the seven trumpets.* prepared themselves to *sound the seven trumpets.* (7) And

Music: Now and Then

the first angel sounded the trumpet, and there followed hail and fire, etc. (8) *And the second angel sounded the trumpet:* and as it were a great mountain, burning with fire, etc. (10) And *the third angel sounded the trumpet*, and a great star fell from heaven. (12) And *the fourth angel sounded the trumpet*, and the third part of the sun was smitten, etc. (13) And I beheld, and heard the voice of one eagle ... saying with a loud voice: Woe, woe, woe to the inhabitants of the earth: by reason of the rest of the voices of the *three angels, who are yet to sound the trumpet*. (Apoc. 9:1): And the *fifth angel sounded the trumpet*, and I saw a star fall, etc. (13) And the *sixth angel sounded the trumpet:* and I heard a voice ... saying to the sixth angel who had the trumpet: Loose the four angels, who are bound in the great river Euphrates."

(Apoc. 10:7): "But in the days of *the voice of the seventh angel, when he shall begin to sound the trumpet,* the mystery of God shall be finished."

St. John's visions of the final days had their counterpart in both the prophetic words of St. Paul and Christ himself. In 1st Corinthians: 15:51, 52, St. Paul wrote: "Behold, I tell you a mystery. We shall all indeed rise again: but we shall not all be changed. In a moment, in the twinkling of an eye, at *the last trumpet: for the trumpet shall sound*, and the dead shall rise again incorruptible: and we shall be changed." And, again (1 Thess. 4:15): "For the Lord himself shall come down from heaven ... with the voice of an archangel, and *with the trumpet of God:* and the dead who are in Christ, shall rise first." Both the visions of St. John and the prophetic writing of St. Paul had been previously foretold in Christ's own words, in His warning of the signs to be witnessed before the end of the world (Matt. 24:31): "And he shall send his *angels with a trumpet, and a great voice:* and they shall gather together his elect from the four winds, from the farthest parts of the heavens to the utmost bounds of them."

❧ Instruments in Combination

The descendants of Jubal, "the father of them that play upon the harp and the organs," was also in all probability the father of the modern symphony orchestra, although contemporary usages were scarcely foreshadowed in his time. While *the sound of the trumpet* and *the songs of the singing men* played the most important part in the music of our forebears, there are notable occasions in the Biblical record when combinations of instruments were appropriately used. One of these important events occurred at the time of Saul's anointing as King, 1040 B.C. (I Kings 10:5), and Samuel predicted to him: "After that thou shalt come to the hill of God ... and ... thou shalt meet a company of prophets coming down from the high place, with *a psaltery and timbrel*, and *a pipe*, and *a harp* before them, and they shall be prophesying."

Again we have to fill in a great many of the degrees which inevitably led up to such a casually mentioned

Music: Now and Then

use of music. These presuppose a development in the making and playing of instruments, the music performed, and the purposes and times of performance, from a period antedating Jubal to a time in the neighborhood of one thousand years later. The instruments at Saul's anointing, as we know, included those that were plucked, such as the psaltery and harp; percussion, in the timbrel; and the wood wind, or pipe. The prophets must have been accustomed to their use, and well practiced therein, or they would not have had the temerity to perform on such an important occasion, with the authority their office demanded. And a traditional repertoire, or, at least, manner and method of performance, must have been in existence, or else their sounds would not have carried the tone of conviction and inevitability which must, by its very nature, have accompanied prophesy. These are self-evident facts. *What* the music sounded like, in tonal quality and volume, as well as the music itself, must, fortunately or unfortunately, be left to the imagination. But, again, the imagination must be reinforced with reason and understanding, so that we may know, beyond the shadow of a doubt, that the words of the prophets were enhanced and, indeed, illumined by their musical investiture. Incidentally, this is a subject that Edgar Allan Poe, at a somewhat later period, expounded with eloquence, in essence, in his essay on "The Poetic Principle."

Although David's name is usually associated with singing, the harp, and even with dancing, we read (II Kings 6:5) that before the ark of God, "David and all

Instruments in Combination

Israel *played . . . on all manner of instruments made of wood, on harps and lutes and timbrels and cornets and cymbals.*" This is the greatest diversity of instruments mentioned up to this time (*circa* 1000 B.C.), so we may attribute this notable development to the adventurous musical nature of David, which, as disciplined as it probably was, seems to have been endowed with a spirit of improvisation and experimentation quite unique. That this extemporaneousness did not always lead to happy consequences, we shall see. Its far-reaching influence for good and inspiration, however, should not go unnoticed at this point, although it may only be mentioned in passing. I refer, specifically, to the formation of that brave, imaginary, but nonetheless real, "*Davidsbund*" by the great composer, Robert Schumann, in the first half of the 19th century, A.D. The spirit of fantasy that actuated the music-making of David was reborn many centuries later and became manifest in the creative output of one of our most highly endowed modern composers. It is also worthy of mention that this unique spirit, with its unpredicted and unpredictable flights of fantasy, was not only misunderstood at David's time, but in our own day. So history repeats itself!

From the time of Jubal, and presumably before, as we have seen, various combinations of instruments were in common use, although usually with singing, even, sometimes, with dancing. That they were used traditionally on many unspecified occasions we must assume, as in the instance of the "great marriage" (I Mach. 9:37, 39), "when the bridegroom came forth, and his friends, and his brethren . . . with *timbrels, and musical instruments.*" Festive occasions and music went hand in hand even in those days, although the participation seems to have been more general, not being confined to a special musical group or individual, separate from the guests and principals.

Women in Biblical Music

The mention of women in the music of our forebears of Biblical times occurs with relative infrequency, and never in connection with instituted procedures, either in liturgy, periods of war or intervals of peace. The reason for their virtual non-participation is not explained, nor is it evident. However, it would seem that the important, organized part played by music in the spiritual and physical struggles of our progenitors placed it, automatically, in the category of those occasions, primarily confined to public events, that were under the direct supervision of men. Since women were not ordained as priests, nor were they warriors, it is easily perceived that, in the midst of their other multifarious duties, they seldom had time, opportunity or incentive to become actively a part of early musical procedures or to enter into the institution of traditions. The far-reaching influence of these incontrovertible facts is felt even to our own day, although latterly, along with other "emancipations" which have given them greater latitude, we find more women in music,

Women in Biblical Music

especially in careers in which vanity is the dominating factor. In spite of these considerations, it is recorded that (Exod. 15:20, 21):" Mary the Prophetess, the sister of Aaron, *took a timbrel* in her hand: *and all the women* went forth after her *with timbrels and with dances* ... And *she began the song to them, saying, Let us sing to the Lord*, for he is gloriously magnified." The mere use of the timbrel, which we may think of as a primitive tambourine or easily sounded percussion instrument, together "with dances," does not indicate evidence of organized musical participation by women, either of traditional nature or capable of becoming a tradition. Even at that time, in a moment of joy, it would have been a simple matter gaily to have improvised dancing steps for which the timbrel gave the rhythm. And, as for the song of praise, it will be noted that the words of her canticle were not continued or developed, and that it is specifically stated that she "*began* the song. ... " Evidently Mary the Prophetess' intentions of singing to the Lord were good, but incapable of fulfillment.

The foregoing interpretation of Mary's musical participation, based upon the revised Douay version, may be considered as a "subjective" one. It is! But this particular account has been, and may well be, subject to various interpretations. If one accepts the more literal translation of the word "began," using "answered" in place of "began" as given above, the conclusions may be very different. It has been asserted, for instance, that when "Miriam (Mary) 'answered' (instead of 'began') them: Sing ye to the Lord, for he

Music: Now and Then

hath triumphed gloriously," it was merely evidence of early antiphonal singing, and that her rejoinder was in the nature of a formal response. Even this more "objective" version assumes much. A new and different recounting of Mary's "beginning" or "answering," as the case may be, might assert with equal authority that Mary's answering, which appears to have been only *in part*, other opinions to the contrary notwithstanding, was an outstanding example of woman's predilection for the last word! Anyone, everyone, can take his choice of versions! Such quibblings, if carried out at length and frequently, could only end in losing the spirit of music, on countless occasions, in obscurantism.

Later, we find (Judges 11:34) that the simple timbrel was used similarly, in celebration of victory in battle: "And when Jepthe returned ... to his house, his only daughter met him *with timbrels and dances*." This time, all mention of song is omitted! However, singing was included in the women's joyful greeting in another hour of victory (I Kings 18:6, 7): "When David returned, after he slew the Philistine, the *women* came out ... *singing and dancing*, to meet King Saul, *with timbrels of joy, and cornets*, and *the women sang as they played*, and they said: Saul slew his thousands, and David his ten thousands." Better had their song been silenced! Their ill-chosen words were a perfect example of saying the right thing at the wrong time. What was intended as a joyful greeting to Saul only served to arouse his ire against David, by virtue of the invidious comparison.

Women in Biblical Music

The ill-timed praise of Saul by the playing, singing, and dancing women was not the only time that David was to suffer unforeseen condemnation and injustice, as a direct outgrowth of participation in that for which he had such a strong predilection. When "David . . . brought the Ark of the Covenant of the Lord *with joyful shouting*, and *with sound of trumpet* (II Kings 6: 15–23), and . . . Michol, the daughter of Saul, looking out through a window, saw King David leaping and dancing before the Lord . . . she despised him in her heart.' After David had offered "holocausts and peace offerings, he blessed the people in the name of the Lord of hosts." Then "David returned to bless his own house: and Michol . . . coming out to meet David, said: How glorious was the King of Israel today, uncovering himself before the handmaids of his servants, and was naked, as if one of the buffoons should be naked. And David said to Michol: Before the Lord, who chose me rather than thy father, and than all his house, and commanded me to be ruler over the people of the Lord in Israel, I will both play and make myself meaner than I have done: and I will be little in my own eyes: and with the handmaids of whom thou speakest, I shall appear more glorious." And as a punishment for her imputation of evil to David, in demeaning himself in ecstasy before the Lord, "Michol the daughter of Saul had no child to the day of her death." This is the first record of what is known vulgarly in modern parlance as a "strip tease." But, in this case, the evil lay only in Michol's mind. Her unjust judgment and failure to grasp the significance of David's true mo-

Music: Now and Then

tive in expressing joy before the Lord in ecstatic improvisation, not only resulted in Michol's barrenness, but may, in part at least, account for the general lack of women's participation in music, with the same equality and understanding granted men, even to modern times.

However unhappily women may have been associated with music, we find that at the celebration of the slaying of Holofernes by Judith (Judith 15, 16), "all the people rejoiced ... *playing on instruments and harps* ... Then *Judith sung this canticle* to the Lord, saying: Begin ye to the Lord *with timbrels*, sing ye to the Lord *with cymbals, tune unto him a new psalm. Let us sing a hymn* to the Lord, *let us sing a new hymn* to our God ... And for three months the joy of this victory was celebrated with Judith."

Judith stands out, however, as a most notable exception, not only musically in singing a new hymn of praise to God, but in more sanguinary matters. In both respects she was not typical of her sex, although other exceptions may have appeared from time to time. They only tend to confirm our general contention that, traditionally, women were not participants in music in Biblical times.

Lest we tend towards a pessimistic tone, in appraisal of women's relation to music in earlier days, let us not forget the words of Zacharias, in the midst of his prophecy concerning the coming of Christ: "*Sing* praise, and rejoice, *O Daughter* of Sion: for behold I come, and I will dwell in the midst of thee: saith the Lord." This rainbow on the horizon of women's beclouded musical

Song, Without Instruments

world presaged a relationship to music which, even now, is gradually becoming clearer as the obscuring clouds are dispelled and new vistas are exposed to view.

Song, Without Instruments

Song, in all probability, was implanted in the heart of man and was his most natural mode of musical expression long before the earliest mention of musical instruments in the Bible, at the time of Jubal. As with instrumental music, the earlier references to song presuppose its existence and development to a high degree. What the origins of song were, and the steps that followed, have been the subject of much imaginative speculation, particularly by scientists and philosophers. They have ascribed the first beginnings variously to the biological urge, as in Spencer; to the practical demands of the struggle for existence, as in Bücher. Musicologists have practically ignored this speculative field, and it is interesting to note the generally prevailing avoidance by self-appointed experts of the earliest purpose ascribed to song in the Biblical record: *in praise of God.*

The inspiration for song is found too frequently in connection with occasions for praise and rejoicing, in thanks to the Almighty, to be waived aside for any other considerations, or speculative assumptions. It seems utterly natural and appropriate that (Exod. 15:

Music: Now and Then

1, etc.), when "Moses and the children of Israel *sung this canticle to the Lord:* ... *for he is gloriously magnified.* ... *The Lord is my strength and praise, etc.*," he and the chosen people should lift their voices in song. "This canticle" evidently refers to an already existing song, familiar to the participants. As we shall see, the appearance of an unfamiliar song is specifically referred to as "a *new* canticle."

Indeed, the institution of song as an essential in the spiritual lives of the people is clearly indicated in the words of the Lord to Moses (Deut. 31:19): "Now therefore *write you this canticle,* and *teach the children of Israel: that they may know it by heart, and sing it by mouth, and this song may be unto me a testimony....*"

As the trumpets were used in summoning men to battle and deploying and encouraging them for combat, so song was appropriately used for the celebration of victory, in the canticle of Debbora and Barac (Judges 5): "O you of Israel, that have willingly offered your lives to danger, *bless the Lord.* Hear, O ye Kings, give ear, ye princes: It is I, it is *I, that will sing to the Lord, I will sing to the Lord, the God of Israel.*"

The earliest ballad on record seems to have been Samson's bursting into song, prior to his going single-handed against the Philistines. To give added eloquence to the recounting of his previous deeds of valor to the assembled people, the tale is told that (Judges 15:17): "*When he* (Samson) *had ended these words, singing,* he threw the jawbone out of his hand." The effect of this musico-dramatic narration upon the astounded spectators and the Philistines, must have been

Song, Without Instruments

more electrifying than any achievement in our opera houses, though scarcely to be accorded an encore.

Belief in the efficacy of song, in entreaty to God, was strongly indicated by Mardochai, when he prayed (Esther 13:17): "Hear my supplication, and be merciful to thy lot and inheritance, and turn our mourning into joy, that we may live and praise thy name, O Lord, and *shut not the mouths of them that sing* to thee." And, from the depths of his despair, Job cried (Job 35): "Where is *God*, who made me, *who hath given songs in the night?*"

Both Mardochai and Job, in moments of darkness, associated song with the Almighty, both in source and potentiality. Such spontaneous outbursts add irrefutable evidence, if that were needed, of the essential part played by music in the thoughts and lives of the ancients. It permeated their whole existence; it was not only on their lips but in the innermost recesses of their being. It was not a plaything for moments of leisure and relaxation, but an indissoluble connection with the very sources of being — the Almighty! It was a supernatural manifestation of God's spirit in the soul of man, becoming articulate through the physical bounty with which man has been endowed.

The occasions for song were as varied and diversified as the reasons for man's offering praise to God. (Wisdom 10:19, 20) "Therefore the just took the spoils of the wicked. And *they sung to thy holy name, O Lord.*" And Isaias (Isaias 26) commanded that a canticle of thanks be offered for the delivery of God's people, saying: "In that day *shall this canticle be sung* in the land

Music: Now and Then

of Juda." Isaias' song, following the command, was an exalted blending of praise and prophecy which must have been pleasing to the Almighty, as it was inspiring to the people.

The eloquence of Isaias' words undoubtedly resounded with overwhelming effect when invested with music. That the prophet had a profound belief in the power of song is expressed in rarely poetic, metaphorical imagery (Isaias 30:29): "You shall have a song as in the night of the sanctified solemnity, and joy of heart, *as when one goeth with a pipe* to come into the mountain of the Lord, to the Mighty One of Israel."

This is not the only Biblical reference to song "in the night." The poetry implicit in the idea of music rising from the depths of darkness may well have been the inspiration for Chopin's Nocturnes.

On occasion, Isaias' exaltation demanded an extemporaneous musical outburst (Isaias 42:10): "*Sing to the Lord a new song*, his praise is from the ends of the earth: you that go down to the sea, and all that are therein: ye islands, and ye inhabitants of them. Let the desert and the cities thereof be exalted."

However, Isaias did not merely confine his singing to the more exalted moments of praise and prophecy, as we find in his delivery of a parable, foreshowing the reprobation of the Jews because of their sins (Isaias 5): "*I will sing to my beloved the canticle of* my cousin concerning his vineyard. My beloved had a vineyard on a hill in a fruitful place, etc. etc."

Both Isaias and Jeremias were characterized by a spontaneous, inspired use of song, thereby giving flight

Abuse of Music; and in Lamentation

to moments of exaltation and ecstasy, in contrast to the carefully and thoroughly organized use of liturgical music. Typical of Isaias is the outburst (Isaias 54:1): "*Sing forth praise, and make a joyful noise,*" and, similarly (Jer. 20:13), Jeremias': "*Sing ye to the Lord, praise the Lord.*" And, according to Jeremias (Jer. 31:7) "... thus saith the Lord: Rejoice ye in the joy of Jacob ...: *shout ye, and sing.*"

The voice of prophecy was also the voice of song. Praise from the lips of these giants of antiquity soared to heaven on wings of song. Their warnings, commands, as well as words of encouragement and faith, carried to the people with a significance incapable to realization by the spoken word alone. Realizing the tremendous God-given power of song in unifying people in common emotion, Jeremias was inspired to impute to the Almighty himself, the injunction: "*Shout ye, and sing.*" (Jer. 31:7).

✧ Abuse of Music; and in Lamentation

God's intentions were clearly that music should be used for the benefit of mankind and for His praise and glory. Yet, as in numerous other deviations from clearly delineated policy and divine injunction, music was sometimes used for other than established purposes.

An early instance of abuse of music is related in connection with idolatry (Exod. 32:17, 19), when Josue

Music: Now and Then

said to Moses: "The noise of battle is heard in the camp. But he (Moses) answered: It is not the cry of men encouraging to fight, nor the shout of men compelling to flee: but *I hear the voice of singers.* And when he came close to the camp *he saw the calf,* and *the dances:* and he was very angry." So was music "Crucified on a cross of gold."

Job, in wonder and lament over the apparent prosperity of the sinful rich, even as we unto this day, cried (Job 21:7): "Why do the wicked live, are they advanced and strengthened with riches? . . . (12) *They take the timbrel and the harp, and rejoice at the sound of the organ.*" And, bemoaning the great change in his temporal state, from welfare to calamity, Job is impelled to observe (Job 30:9): "*Now I am turned into their* (the people's) *song, and am become their byword* . . . (31) *My harp is turned to mourning, and my organ into the voice of those that weep.*" Tchaikovsky seems to have fallen heir to this latter mood, and it remains perhaps the most revealing insight into the depths of despair into which both Job and the modern master fell, although for very different reasons.

A philosophical note was injected, by the author of Ecclesiasticus (22:6), in the sage observation: "A tale out of time is like *music in mourning:* but the stripes and instructions of wisdom are never out of time."

Isaias had other cause for complaint in the lament (Isaias 5:11, 12): "Woe unto you that rise up early in the morning to follow drunkenness. *The harp and the lyre, and the timbrel, and the pipe,* and wine are in your feasts." And later, Isaias, prophesying depths of degra-

Abuse of Music; and in Lamentation

dation into which music could fall (Isaias 23:15): "And it shall come to pass in that day that thou, O Tyre, shalt be forgotten, seventy years, ... but after seventy years, there shall be unto Tyre *as the song of a harlot.* (16) *Take a harp,* go about the city, thou harlot (Tyre) that hast been forgotten: *sing well, sing many a song, that thou mayest be remembered.*" This latter phrase may well have been the inspiration for Robert Louis Stevenson's "Sing me a song of a lad that is gone; Say, could that lad be I?" The difference between general and individual application of this "song of remembrance," is merely the difference between times and places: between the "classic" and "romantic," so-called; between the universal and the personal!

Those who listen to the eloquence of preachers, even hear the word of God, and, revelling in mere sound, as of a song, and heed not, existed, even at the time of Ezechiel (Ezech. 33:30, 31, 32): "And thou son of man: the children of thy people, ... one to another, each man to his neighbor, saying: Come, let us hear what is the word that cometh forth from the Lord. And they come to thee ... and hear thy words, and do them not: *for they turn them into a song of their mouth* ... And thou art to them *as a musical song which is sung with a sweet and agreeable voice:* and they hear thy words, and do them not." Even "lip service" may be given added sweetness and eloquence by virtue of song but its emptiness remains uncloaked! Separated from its proper sphere, music only adds a specious element to words and the sum total is futility.

Music: Now and Then

A story made familiar, in part only, by a modern, popular song, if not by the complete scriptural account, is that of the worship of Nabuchodonosor's golden calf, in which music was intended to play an important role. Here, again, is a demonstration of the failure of music to add to an occasion, when its true potentialities are ignored and its functions are abased. (Dan. 3:4, 5): "Then a herald cried with a strong voice: To you it is commanded, O nations, tribes and languages: That in the hour that you shall hear *the sound of the trumpet, and of the flute, and of the harp, of the sackbut, and of the psaltery, and of the symphony, and of all kind of music;* ye fall down and adore ... the golden statue which King Nabuchodonosor hath set up. (7) Upon this therefore, at the time when all the people heard *the sound of the trumpet, the flute, and the harp, of the sackbut, and the psaltery, and the symphony and of all kind of music* ... they fell down and adored."

Then, the Chaldeans, accusing the Jews, said (Dan. 3:10): "Thou, O King, hast made a decree that every man that shall hear *the sound of the trumpet, the flute, and the harp, of the sackbut, and the psaltery, of the symphony, and of all kind of music*, shall prostrate himself, and adore the golden statue. (11) And if any man shall not fall down and adore, he shall be cast into a furnace of burning fire." The failure of Sidrach, Misach and Abdenago to become idolators, even to the accompaniment of such an hitherto unparalleled assemblage of musical instruments, in fact, a veritable "symphony," graphically depicts the emptiness, even the anticlimax that may be produced by an instrumental barrage when

Abuse of Music; and in Lamentation

not used for the glory of God — for high ideals. Even some of our most famous modern composers, in creating a tower of Babel in sound, have forgotten this lesson in futility, in their failure to realize that "orchestration is not music." Our modern ears can well imagine the terrific din invoked by the early "symphony," whose formula, "The more platitudinous: the louder," is all too familiar.

In the resounding words of the prophets are sometimes to be found allusions to musical developments, even unto our own day. The desolation of Israel for their pride and luxury, was foretold by Amos in terms which may well describe the presumption of contemporary creative musicians who have squandered their heritage, in sublimating musical ideas to the luxury of instrumental sounds, as though the latter were a divinely instituted tradition (Amos 6:5): "You that *sing to the sound of the psaltery: they have thought themselves to have instruments of music like David.*" The essential difference lay not in the utilization of the instruments but in the sources of inspiration and the purpose for which music was used. Surely David's inspiring musical influence could not be perpetuated merely by the "bigger and better" effects of those who "thought themselves to have instruments like David."

While music served mankind in praise of God and in strengthening his followers in the various struggles that were their lot, there is ample evidence of its added eloquence and ennobling influence in the hour of grief. Even Jeremias, whose ability to express sorrow in words seems to have no limitations, had recourse to music to

Music: Now and Then

express the very extremity of grief at the time of the death of Josias: (II Par. 35:24, 25): " ... and all Juda and Jerusalem mourned for him, particularly *Jeremias: whose lamentations* for Josias *all the singing men and all the singing women* repeat unto this day."

Isaias, moved to warn the people of the judgments of God to be visited upon wrong doers, envisions the very depths of woe as a world of sin from which the joys of music have vanished (Isaias 24:8): "*The mirth of timbrels* hath ceased, *the noise of them that rejoice* is ended, *the melody of the harp* is silent. (9) They shall not drink wine *with a song.*" Even the luxury of musical lamentation is to be denied people in the depths of despair because of sin, in the direful warnings of Isaias. Similar desolation of a people and one of the greatest of punishments were foretold by Jeremias, in prophesying the seventy years' captivity preceding the fall of Babylon (Jer. 25:10): "And I will take away from them *the voice of mirth*, and *the voice of gladness*, and *the voice of the bride, etc.*" But with the restoration of Israel, Jeremias promised the return of "*praise in Mount Sion*" (Jer. 31:12, 13): "Then shall the virgin *rejoice in the dance.*" And (15) "Rachel weeping for her children, and refusing to be comforted," heard the reassuring words of the Lord (16): "Let thy voice cease from weeping, and thy eyes from tears: for there is reward for thy work, saith the Lord: and they shall return out of the land of the enemy."

God's blessings upon the release of the Israelites from the desolation of a captivity in which "the voice of mirth, the voice of gladness" were no longer heard,

Abuse of Music; and in Lamentation

included the promise of a return of the joyful sounds of music. That the references to "voice of mirth and of gladness," applied to singing is safely to be assumed, inasmuch as the Levites, traditionally God's ministers in duly appointed charge of liturgical singing, were specifically mentioned (Jer. 33:18) in this connection.

Again, in Jeremias' prophecy of the desolation of Moab (Jer. 48), because of its pride, the Almighty said (33): "Joy and gladness is taken away from Carmel, and from the land of Moab, and I have taken away the wine out of the presses: the treader of the grapes *shall not sing the accustomed cheerful tune.* . . . (36) Therefore (saith the Lord) *my heart shall sound for Moab like pipes . . .* " Songs of grief were an appropriate accompaniment to lamentation, but no more direful punishment to sinful people, whether Israelites or Moabites, could be inflicted upon them, than the silencing of songs of joy and gladness: of praise to God. This was the very depths of desolation! Even the physical evidences of participation in music were removed from Jerusalem, at the time of its looting by the Chaldeans (Jer. 52:18): "And they took the caldrons, and the flesh hooks, and *the psalteries*, and the bowls, and the little mortars, and all the brazen vessels *that had been used in the ministry*, etc."

Jeremias, lamenting the miseries of his people (Lam. of Jer. 3:14), cried: "I am made a derision to all my people, *their song all the day long.*" And, again, he bewails (63): "*I am their song.*" Evidently Jeremias would have preferred not to have been committed to people's memory in song. It served only to add to his grief. At

Music: Now and Then

least he was saved the torture of radio broadcasts of his misery, and its being reproduced, in "indestructible" form, on records. Such negative blessings were not, alas, rainbows on the horizon of his grief!

Jeremias' final outburst, in prayer, recounts the complete desolation of his people, in the midst of pleas for salvation (Lam. of Jer. 5:14, 15): "the young men (have ceased) *from the choir of singers.* The joy of our heart is ceased, *our dancing is turned into mourning.*"

David added the eloquence of his voice (Ps. 136), in a psalm "for Jeremias," "a lamentation of the people of God in their captivity in Babylon:" "Upon the rivers of Babylon, there we sat and wept... On the willows in the midst thereof *we hung up our instruments.* For there they that led us into captivity required of us the *words of songs.* And they that carried us away, said: *Sing ye to us a hymn of the songs of Sion. How shall we sing the song of the Lord* in a strange land?" The voice that customarily was raised in joy and praise of God was silent, midst the grief of captivity.

With Ezechiel, as with Jeremias, music as lamentation, as well as the desolation of a world in which music was no longer heard, played an important part in prophecy. Foretelling the destruction of Tyre, in the words of the Lord, he said (Ezech. 26:13): "I will make *the multitude of thy songs to cease,* and *the sound of thy harps shall be heard no more:*"... And (Ezech. 27:32) they shall take up *a mournful song* for thee, and shall lament thee: What city is like Tyre, *which is become silent* in the midst of the sea?" In like manner

Abuse of Music; and in Lamentation

Ezechiel lamented the fall of the King of Egypt (Ezech. 32:17, 18): "the word of the Lord came to me saying: Son of man, *sing a mournful song* for the multitude of Egypt."

The tradition of prophecy in song, especially in expressing despair over God's punishments of the people for sin, and disregard of their duties and obligations to the Almighty, was continued by Amos in his lamentation for Israel (Amos 5:1, 21, 23): "The house of Israel is fallen ... (saith the Lord) I hate, and have rejected your festivities. ... Take away from me *the tumult of thy songs: and I will not hear the canticles of thy harp.*" (Amos 8:10) "And *I will turn your feasts into mourning and all your songs into lamentation.*"

The greatest potency in describing the depths of desolation into which an afflicted people could fall, when they incurred God's wrath, was ascribed to music, either in lamentations, withdrawal of the blessings of music, turning joyful song into grief, or the refusal of God to receive musical offerings. The frequency with which these various and dire punishments are attributed, not to one of the prophets particularly given to lamenting, such as Jeremias, but to many of the spiritual leaders of the Old Testament, conclusively proves the divinely endowed nature of music. One does not need to have recourse to Biblical records to realize the infamy visited upon the abasement of music. However, with the dominance of commercialized music in our lives, the occasions of its misuse are so frequent and flagrant, that we have become accustomed and inured to a degradation that, in olden times, was of relative

Music: Now and Then

infrequency — hence more direful in implications of doom.

In fulfillment of the prophetic tradition, Micheas (to the Israelites) (Mich. 2:4) warned: "(thus saith the Lord): In that day (i.e. the day of punishment for sins) a parable shall be taken up upon you, and *a song shall be sung with melody* by them that say: We are laid waste and spoiled, etc."

At a time much closer to the coming of Christ (*circa* 175–136 B.C.), we find Judas Machabeus, in speaking of the desolation of Jerusalem, employing the same terminology used by the prophets in giving emphasis to warnings of punishment for offenses (1 Mach. 3:45): "... and joy was taken away from Jacob, and the *pipe and harp ceased* there." Similarly, in repetition of another familiar transmutation of music from purposes of praise and joy, it is recounted that, when Jonathan sought to avenge the wanton murder of his brother John, marriage festivities (I Mach. 9:41) were "turned into mourning, and the *noise of their musical instruments* into lamentation."

With the coming of Christ and the advent of a new order, there is a natural break in the continuity of references to customary, traditional musical usages. Before music was reorganized by the Christian church and became attuned to new demands and institutions, there is evidence that it was still a necessary function in time of lamentation (Matt. 9:23), as when the daughter of a ruler lay dead, and Jesus "*saw the minstrels* and the multitude making a rout."

And, in the parable of the prodigal son, Jesus spoke

of the resentment aroused in the elder son (Luke 15: 25), when "he came nigh to the house" and "heard *music and dancing*." In that instance, music which served in joyful celebration for the many, intensified the grief of one. Consumed by evil emotions, he remained outside the magic spell of music. It is not an uncommon experience. Many, in the depths of self, remain impervious to the joys of music, on many an otherwise happy occasion.

In admonishing the people for their unbelief, both in prophecy and fulfillment, Christ said (Matt. 11:15–17): "He that hath ears to hear, let him hear. But whereunto shall I esteem this generation to be like? It is like children sitting in the market place. Who crying to their companions say: *We have piped to you, and you have not danced:* we have lamented, and you have not mourned." St. Luke (7:32) used these identical words. The analogy was a powerful one: the failure of those who had heard the prophetic words of John the Baptist and the more ancient prophets, and believed not; who also, as it were, hearing music, were incapable of appropriate response. Their number is still legion. "Ears they have, and they hear not!"

There are many evidences that St. Paul was musical, but one, in particular, that he must have suffered at some time from bad intonation. This is implicit in the querulous tone of (I Cor. 14:7): "Even things without life that give *sound*, whether *pipe or harp*, except they give a *distinction of sounds*, how shall it be known what is *piped or harped?*"

Using the analogy of the fall of Babylon, envisaging

Music: Now and Then

the desolation of those to whom judgment and punishment are to be meted out in the final day, St. John (Apoc. 18:22) foretold: "And *the voice of harpers, and of musicians*, and of *them that play on the pipe, and on the trumpet, shall be heard no more* at all in thee."

Thomas a' Kempis ("Imitation of Christ") continues the direful, allegorical picture of cataclysmic destruction in the words: "For *in that last hour*, all shall perish: castles, cities, villages, vessels of gold and silver, etc. . . . Then *shall be mute, lyre, trumpet, pipe and harp*. There shall be . . . *no more dance nor shouting, nor more songs* . . . for the hearts of all shall wither away, and the whole earth shall tremble in the presence of God."

Song, With Instruments

We are so accustomed to associate the early combination of song and instruments with relatively modern minstrelsy, that the frequent allusions to its common usage in Biblical times are generally disregarded. Indisputable evidence attests customary performance of song with instrumental accompaniment, both on more ordinary occasions and those clearly instituted by the Almighty for His worship.

Again, we come upon the record of a specific event that presupposes the existence of long established custom and practice. And again, we can only conjecture the length of time such custom had been in existence,

Song, With Instruments

how long it had been in formation, the quality and capacities of instruments, how the music itself sounded, etc. It is indeed a fertile field for conjecture. But "conjecture" it remains, and one man's guess is probably as good as another's; but variable in diversity and extent with each one's capacity for imagination and experience. However, when one considers what a vast number of tomes might result, if this musical no-man's-land were opened up to musicologists, it is just as well that we are spared such additional weariness to the already afflicted flesh.

The Biblical accounts, in spite of lack of other data, are sufficiently graphic and sometimes detailed, that we may adduce adequate facts to establish what is of primary interest to us in this investigation: the instruments employed; the various usages of music with the ancients; the spirit of occasions for its use, which were indubitably enhanced by music; the existence of music in common use in connection with daily events in the lives of the people; the last, but not least, the institution of liturgical music.

To return to the record of "a specific event" mentioned in early Biblical history, we find Laban saying to Jacob (Gen. 31:27) "Why wouldst thou run away privately and not acquaint me, that I might have brought thee on the way *with joy*, and *with songs, timbrels*, and *with harps?*" Music as an appropriate farewell far antedated the composition of Bach's "Capriccio on the Departure of a Beloved Brother" or Beethoven's "Les Adieux" Sonata, although these latter are subjected to more oft-repeated performance.

Music: Now and Then

Probably it is more commonly known, or perhaps "recalled" is a more accurate word, that the directions and specifications for the building of the Ark of the Covenant and the Temple are given in the Old Testament, than that music was so definitely instituted for liturgical usage. And, lest it be assumed that David excelled to such high degree in inventiveness and the spirit of extemporaneousness, that he is to be remembered primarily in connection with fantasy, let it be observed, without possibility of disregarding a most important fact in the annals of music: that David was responsible for the organization and expansion of music in the lives of the people, for the highest ideals, aims and usages.

The importance of the function of music in the worship of God is manifested in the appointment of Levites to fulfill all duly instituted musical procedures. David had already said (I Par. 15:2): "No one ought to carry the ark of God, but the Levites, whom the Lord hath chosen to carry it, and to minister unto himself forever." So it was to these ministers of the Almighty that David entrusted the sacred institutions of music in worship (I Par. 15:16): "And *David spoke to the chiefs of the Levites, to appoint some of their brethren to be singers with musical instruments, to wit, on psalteries, and harps, and cymbals,* that the joyful noise might resound on high." The Biblical account continues with the enumeration of those appointed.

Not only were the Levites delegated to sing and play before the Ark of the Covenant, but the functions and organization of the musical ministers, in groups, was

Song, With Instruments

specified (19): "Now *the singers*, Hemam, Asaph, and Ethan, *sounded with cymbals of brass*. (20) And Zacharias, and Oziel, and Semiramoth, and Jehiel, and Ani, and Eliab, and Maasias, and Banaias, *sung mysteries upon psalteries*. (21) And Mathathias, and Eliphalu, and Macenias and Obededom, and Jehiel and Ozaziu, *sung a song of victory for the octave upon harps*. (22) And *Chonenias chief of the Levites, presided over the prophecy, to give out the tunes: for he was very skilful*." Yet others, among them certain priests, were designated "*to sound with trumpets*" (I Par. 15:24) . . . "before the ark of God."

David, however, was not content to relegate musical participation to the duly appointed ministers, but was inspired to join with them (I Par. 15:27): "And David was clothed with a robe of fine linen, and all the Levites that carried the ark, and *the singing men*, and *Chonenias the ruler of the prophecy among the singers:* and David also had on him an ephod of linen. (28) And all Israel brought the ark of the covenant of the Lord *with joyful shouting, and sounding with the sound of the cornet, and with trumpets, and cymbals, and psalteries, and harps*." This was indeed a glorious occasion, a climax for David and the people in God's worship. The only anti-climactic note injected into this history-making event was the failure of Michol, David's wife, to enter into the spirit of the occasion. Since this has been duly considered here, under the caption "*Women in Music*," it is only to be observed, in passing, that Michol seems to have been the prototype for a larger number of present-day listeners, who, as it were, observe

Music: Now and Then

"from a window," seldom, if ever, entering into the true spirit of a musical occasion.

When the Ark was placed in the tabernacle, the musical ordinance was continued (I Par. 16:4-6), with the Levites "ministering before the ark of the Lord, and to remember his works, and to glorify, and praise the Lord God of Israel. *Asaph the chief*, and next after him Zacharias: moreover Jahiel, and Semiramoth, and Jehiel, and Mathathias, and Eliab, and Banaias, and Obededom: and Jehiel over *the instruments of psaltery, and harps:* and *Asaph sounded with cymbals*. But Banaias, and Jaziel the priests, *to sound the trumpet continually* before the ark of the covenant of the Lord."(7) "And in that day *David made Asaph the chief to give praise to the Lord with his brethren* . . . (9) *Sing to him, yea, sing praises to him:* and relate all his wondrous works" . . . (42) "And Heman and Idithun *sounded the trumpet, and played on the cymbals, and all kinds of musical instruments to sing praises to God.*"

Later, when David "was old and full of days (I Par. 23:1) and made Solomon his son King over Israel," he said (25): "The Lord the God of Israel hath given rest to his people, and a habitation in Jerusalem forever . . . (27) So according to the last precepts of David, the *sons of Levi* are to be numbered from twenty years old and upward. (28) And they are to be *under the hand of the sons of Aaron* for service of the house of the Lord . . . in all the works of the ministry of the temple of the Lord . . . (30) *And the Levites are to stand in the morning to give thanks, and to sing praises to the Lord: and in like manner in the evening.* (31) As well in the oblation of

Song, With Instruments

the holocausts of the Lord, as in the sabbaths and in the new moons, and the rest of the solemnities, according to the number and ceremonies prescribed for everything, *continually* before the Lord. (32) And let them keep the observances of the tabernacle of the covenant, and the ceremonies of the sanctuary, and the charge of the sons of Aaron their brethren (under whom the Levites, ministers of God and the singing men, were), that they may minister in the house of the Lord."

Certainly the institution and definite delineation of musical procedures, for divine purpose, by rulers of the people, seems strange to us in A.D. 1955. But it must be recalled, if possible, that this occurred before "separation of Church and State"* had become a tragic fact. Still more difficult to envisage is a time in the affairs of man, when worship and praise of the Almighty were considered essential to temporal welfare as well as eternal salvation, when, in truth, "Church and State"* were indivisible. It is indeed less taxing to our limited comprehensions, to sense an evanescent security when we read that a present-day ruler "attended church on Sunday," when not on a cruise with friends on the official yacht; and to imagine a romantic aura about the official residence that houses the head of his party, who as relaxation from affairs of state, found relief in playing Beethoven's "Minuet in G," or, nostalgically, had recourse to the "Missouri Waltz."

But to return to the story of the ordering and division of musicians by David! This is given in great detail

* This reference is historical, without relation to the necessary separation of Church and State which we enjoy in America.

Music: Now and Then

in the 25th chapter of the 1st Paralipomenon (sometimes known as Chronicles), far too great to be quoted here. The thoroughness of the organization might well provide Petrillo with some untried ideas, in case he needs any! It is sufficient for our purposes to quote the general plan (I Par. 25:1, etc.): "Moreover David and the chief officers of the army separated for the ministry the *sons of Asaph, and of Heman, and of Idithun: to prophesy with harps, and with psalteries, and with cymbals*, according to their number serving in their appointed office." In addition to the listing of the names of those designated "for the service of the house of the Lord" with music, with various instruments and song specifically ordained, it is of particular interest to read that a procedure so definitely established was to be furthered, maintained and preserved as a tradition through duly appointed instructors (I Par. 25:7, etc.): "And the number of them with their brethren, *that taught the song of the Lord, all the teachers*, were two hundred and eighty-eight. And they cast lots by their courses, the elder equally with the younger, the learned and the unlearned together — etc."

Not only were the divisions, deploying, specific duties of each group ordered, but it was clearly established that the services were instituted for general participation, including, even, the King (I Par. 25:5, 6): "(Following a list of names) All these were the sons of Heman the seer of the King in the words of God, *to lift up the horn:* and God gave Heman fourteen sons and three daughters. *All these* under their father's hand *were distributed to sing in the temple of the Lord, with cymbals,*

Song, With Instruments

and psalteries and harps, for the service of the house of the Lord *near the King:* to wit, *Asaph* (in charge of 'prophesying'), and Idithun (who with his sons '*prophesied with a harp* to give thanks and praise to the Lord), and Heman (*who with his sons and daughters sang, with diverse instruments,* 'near the King!'"

Solomon worthily maintained and expanded the tradition instituted by his father, David. At the time of the bringing of the ark into the temple, and the temple was filled with the glory of God (II Par. 5): (1) "Solomon brought in all the things that David his father had vowed, the silver, and the gold, and all the vessels he put among the treasures of the house of God. (2) And after this he gathered together the ancients of Israel, and all the princes of the tribes, and the heads of the families ... And all the men of Israel came to the King in the solemn day of the seventh month. (4) And ... the Levites took up the ark (5) And brought it in ... And the priests with the Levites carried the vessels of the sanctuary ... (6) And King Solomon and all the assembly of Israel, and all that were gathered together before the ark, sacrificed rams, and oxen without number: so great was the multitude of victims ... (11) Now when the priests were come out of the sanctuary ... (12) *Both the Levites and the singing men,* that is, both they that were *under Asaph,* and they that were *under Heman,* and they that were *under Idithun,* with their sons, and their brethren, clothed with fine linen, *sounded with cymbals, and psalteries, and harps* standing on the east side of the altar, and with them *a hundred and twenty priests, sounding with trumpets*

Music: Now and Then

(13) And *when they all sounded together, both with trumpets, and voice, and cymbals, and organs, and with divers kinds of musical instruments, and lifted up their voices on high: the sound was heard afar off,* so that when they began to praise the Lord, and to say: Give glory to the Lord for he is good, for his mercy endureth forever: the house of God was filled with a cloud. (14) Nor could the priests stand and minister by reason of the cloud. For the glory of the Lord had filled the house of God."

After this unparalleled musical fulfillment to the praise and glory of the Almighty, it seems anti-climactic to prolong the recounting of the use of vocal and instrumental music in Biblical times. But such historic heights could not always be maintained, even though a tradition was perpetuated by those who followed David. And many are the evidences of the preservation of musical usages on various occasions.

"When the Queen of Saba heard of the fame of Solomon" (II Par. 9:1), she came to Jerusalem "to see for herself." Having seen the wonders, (3) "to wit, the wisdom of Solomon, and the house which he had built . . . : (4) there was no more spirit in her, she was so astonished." In the interchange of fabulous gifts that followed, among other precious substances and articles that Solomon lavished upon the Queen were "*harps and psalteries for the singing men*" (II Par. 9:11), made from "thyine trees . . . never were there seen such trees in the land of Juda."

The musical tradition established by David in the worship of God, and maintained and expanded by Sol-

Song, With Instruments

omon, was continued by their successors. It was not merely in repetition of the ordinances, but in their renewal, that Asa, three generations after Solomon, in making a solemn covenant with God, with the people (II Par. 15:14): "swore to the Lord *with a loud voice with joyful shouting, and with sound of trumpet, and sound of cornets.*"

The use of more diversified instruments in liturgical music also had influence upon festival occasions, such as the crowning of Joas as King (II Par. 23:12, 13): "When Athalia heard the noise of the people running and praising the King ... and when she saw the King standing upon the step in the entrance (of the temple), and the princes, and the companies about him, and *all the people* of the land *rejoicing, and sounding with trumpets, and playing upon instruments of divers kinds, and the voice of those that praised*, she rent her garments, and said: Treason, treason."

The course of religious worship, however, did not continue without deviations from instituted procedures and true objectives. But when prophets and rulers arose to bring the people back to the worship of God, we find the ordinance of liturgical music playing an important part in the purification of the temple and in the restoration of religion. After the temple had been cleansed and sanctified by Ezechias (II Par. 29), "he (25) *set the Levites* in the house of the Lord *with cymbals, and psalteries, and harps according to the regulation of David the King*, and of God the seer, and of Nathan the prophet, *for it was the commandment of the Lord by the hand of his prophets.* (26) And *the Levites stood, with*

Music: Now and Then

the instruments of David, and the priests with trumpets. (27) ... and when the holocausts were offered, *they began to sing praises to the Lord, and to sound with trumpets, and divers instruments which David the King of Israel had prepared.* (28) And all the multitude adored, and *the singers, and the trumpeters, were in their office* till the holocaust was finished ... (35) and the service of the house of the Lord was completed. (36) And all the people rejoiced because the ministry of the Lord was accomplished. For the resolution of doing this thing was taken suddenly." Evidently the Levites had kept themselves in readiness for this unexpected event, even though the people had wandered for a time from their religious obligations.

Having reestablished the worship of God as instituted by David, Ezechias observed the liturgical celebrations with all possible regularity and meticulous care. For the pasch, he "sent to all Israel and Juda (II Par. 30:1): and he wrote letters to Ephraim and Menasses, that they should come to the house of the Lord in Jerusalem, and keep the phase to the Lord the God of Israel." Although, because of the aforementioned defections from true worship, they could not keep the pasch at its regularly appointed time, Ezechias was again equal to the occasion, and finally enough priests were sanctified, the people gathered, and (II Par. 30:21) "the children of Israel ... kept the feast of unleavened bread seven days with great joy, praising the Lord every day: *the Levites also, and the priests, with instruments that agreed to their office.* (26) And there was a great solemnity in Jerusalem, such as had not been in

Song, With Instruments

that city since the time of Solomon the son of David King of Israel (27) And the priests and *Levites* rose up and blessed the people: and *their voice was heard:* and their prayer came to the holy dwelling place of heaven."

With his purge of the temple and the reestablishment of liturgical worship, Ezechias's crusade against idolatry was by no means ended. As in the maintenance and perpetuation of every true tradition, changing conditions demanded extension of ordinances to meet them. So, after the belated celebration of the pasch (II Par. 31:1) "all Israel . . . went out, and they broke the idols, and cut down the groves, demolished the high places, and destroyed the altars . . . (2) And Ezechias appointed companies of the priests, and *the Levites . . . every man in his own office . . .* to minister, and *to praise, and to sing* in the gates of the camp of the Lord."

Another period of turbulence succeeded the passing of Ezechias, and the Israelites again fell into idolatry and its accompanying evils and desecrations. And again, the Levites rendered new and unfamiliar service at the time of the repairing of the temple by Josias. After ruthlessly purging the temple and killing the idolatrous priests and burning their bones on the altars where they had wickedly sacrificed, Josias faithfully set out "to repair the temple, and mend all that was weak (II Par. 34:10)." Among "the overseers of the workmen were many who hastened the work," and, among these, strangely enough, were "*all Levites skilful to play on instruments.*"

Josias was indeed worthy of his lineage, and, after

Music: Now and Then

many tribulations which he met and overcame with supreme courage and God-given strength, he turned to the established worship of the Almighty, in the celebration of the phase (II Par. 35:1) "on the fourteenth day of the first month." Commanding the people to prepare themselves by their houses and families, (4) "as David King of Israel commanded, and Solomon his son had written," he directed (5) that the sons of Levi should serve in the sanctuary (14): "wherefore the *Levites prepared* ... (15) *And the singers the sons of Asaph stood in their order, according to the commandment of David, and Asaph, and Heman, and Idithun the prophets of the King:* and the porters kept guard at every gate, so as not to depart one moment from their service ... (18) And there was no phase like to this in Israel, from the days of Samuel the prophet: neither did any of all the Kings of Israel keep such a phase as Josias kept, with the priests, and *the Levites*, and all Juda, and Israel that were found, and the inhabitants of Jerusalem."

When Cyrus, King of Persia, released God's people from Babylonian captivity (538 B.C.), and the temple was restored in Jerusalem, *"the singing men and the singing women"* (I Esd. 2:65) were mentioned among those who returned. (70) "So the priests and *the Levites*, and some of the people, and *the singing men* ... dwelt in their cities, and all Israel in their cities." Throughout their captivity, the Levites had been saved as a group, so that they resumed their office without the necessity of time-consuming reorganization and reconsecration. (I Esd. 3:10): "And when the masons laid the foun-

Song, With Instruments

dations of the temple of the Lord, the *priests stood* in their ornaments *with trumpets:* and *the Levites* the sons of Asaph *with cymbals, to praise God by the hands of David king of Israel."* The joy of the people at the restoration of the temple was so overwhelming that (I Esd. 3:12, 13): "When they had the foundation of this temple before their eyes, (they) wept with a loud voice: and many shouting for joy, lifted up their voice. So that one could not distinguish the voice of the shout of joy, from the noise of the weeping of the people: for one with another the people shouted with a loud shout, and the voice was heard afar off." When the temple was completed, the Levites were able, however, to function in their regular office, without their voices being drowned out by such justifiable, spontaneous outbursts as those which greeted the laying of the foundation. (I Esd. 6): (16) "And the children of Israel, the priests and *the Levites,* and the rest of the children of the captivity kept the dedication of the house of God with joy. (18) And they set the priests in their divisions, and *the Levites in their* courses over the works of God in Jerusalem, *as it is written in the book of Moses.* (20) For all the priests *and the Levites were purified as one man."*

The extraordinary importance attached to the services of the Levites, the singing men, both in established worship, as well as in unforeseen emergencies and on special occasions, explains their having been kept intact as a group, even during captivity. It is not surprising, then, to find Artaxerxes the King, issuing a decree to "the keepers of the public chest" that (I Esd. 7:21) "whatsoever Esdras the priest, the scribe of the

Music: Now and Then

law of the God of heaven, shall require of you, you give it without delay. (24) (But) we give you also to understand concerning all the priests, and *the Levites, and the singers . . . that you have no authority to impose toll or tribute, or custom upon them.*"

A sad note, however, is injected into the account of the singing men. We find certain of them numbered among those who fell from favor, and were castigated for their sins in the final chapter of I Esdras, when "Esdras the priest (I Esd. 10:16) and the men heads of the families . . . went and sat down . . . to examine the matter. (17) And they made an end with all the men that had taken strange wives," including (23) certain "*sons of the Levites . . .* and (24) of *the singing men.*" However, let it be said in behalf of the singing men, that their number in this house-cleaning by Esdras, was relatively small!

After the return of the Israelites from the Babylonian captivity, Nehemias, under commission from Artaxerxes, completed the rebuilding of the wall about Jerusalem (446–45 B.C.). (II Esd. 7:1) "Now after the wall was built, and I (Nehemias) had set up the doors, and *numbered the* porters and *singing men, and Levites . . .* (3) And I said to them: Let not the gates of Jerusalem be opened until the sun be hot. And while they were yet standing by, the gates were shut, and barred . . . (5) But God had put in my heart, and I assembled the princes and magistrates, and common people, to number them: and I found a book of the number of them who came up first . . . (6) who came up from the captivity of them that had been carried away, whom Na-

Song, *With Instruments*

buchodonosor the King of Babylon had carried away, and who returned into Judea, everyone to his own city. (73) And the priests, and *the Levites*, and the porters, *and the singing men*, and the rest of the common people, ... and all Israel dwelt in their cities." The Levites, the singing men, it is to be noted, were constantly marked apart, as a special group, never dispersed among other groups or "the common people." Their special protection was the concern of the prophets and rulers, who preserved them for God's service.

When Nehemias made a covenant with God, with the people (II Esd. 10:28, 29), "*the Levites ... and the singing men, and all that had separated themselves from the people of the lands to the law of God,* ... came to promise, and swear that they would walk in the law of God, which he gave in the hand of Moses the servant of God, that they would do and keep all of the commandments of the Lord our God, and his judgments and *ceremonies*." Tithes of all the first fruits of the hands of the people were decreed, to be given the Levites, (38) "and the Levites shall offer the tithe of their tithes in the house of our God ... (39) For the children of Israel and the children of Levi shall carry to the treasury the first fruits of corn, of wine, and of oil: and the sanctified vessels shall be there, and the priests, *and the singing men*, and the porters: and ministers, and we will not forsake the house of our God." Clearly, then, the singing men, whether the occasion be an instituted, ordained procedure, or an extraordinary one, were numbered among the elect!

"At the dedication of the wall of Jerusalem (II Esd.

Music: Now and Then

12:27) they sought *the Levites* out of all their places, to bring them to Jerusalem, and *to keep the dedication*, and *to rejoice with thanksgiving, and with singing, and with cymbals, and psalteries and harps.* (28) And the *sons of the singing men* were gathered together out of the plain country about Jerusalem, and out of the villages ... (29) *for the singing men had built themselves villages round about Jerusalem.*" Again, specific reference is made to the established tradition that "the chief of the Levites (II Esd. 12:24) and their brethren *by their courses, to praise and give thanks according to the commandment of David the man of God*, and to wait equally in order."

By the foregoing, we see the careful, methodical ordering of the favored singing groups, as well as the repetition of their oft-stated primary function: "*to praise and give thanks according to the commandment of David.*" While such divinely instituted procedures and functions never fail to impress us with their great significance, in contemplation of the supreme regard in which music was esteemed by the ancients, the mundane touch in the casual statement that "*the singing men had built themselves villages round about Jerusalem*" gives one pause. Such practical means of relieving congestion, of keeping special groups intact, prepared and available for any and all occasions, not to mention the solicitude shown for their physical well-being, are so remote from present-day musical interests and concern, that one can only marvel!

While the references to the organization of and deploying of the singing men with instruments are both frequent and general, on the occasion of the dedication

Song, With Instruments

of the wall of Jerusalem they are remarkably detailed. (II Esd. 12:30, etc.) It is of particular interest that the formation of the singing forces into "choirs," and their placement, indicated antiphonal singing, with the accompaniment of instruments, on a large scale. At that time, Nehemias "made the princes of Juda go up upon the wall, and ... *appointed two great choirs to give praise.* And they went *on the right hand upon the wall* toward the dunghill gate." After enumerating those who were to follow, Nehemias continues with the ordered sequence of participants, specifically *"the sons of the priests with trumpets,"* with their names, those *"with the musical instruments of David the man of God:* and *Esdras* the scribe *before them at the fountain gate.* And they went up over against them by the stairs of the city of David, at the going up of the wall of the house of David, and *to the water gate eastward:* (37) And *the second choir of them that gave thanks went on the opposite side*, and I after them, and the half of the people upon the wall, and upon the tower of the furnaces, even to the broad wall ... (39) And *the two choirs* of them that *gave praise* stood still at the house of God ... and *the priests ... with trumpets* ... And *the singers sung loud*, and Jezraia was their overseer ... *and they rejoiced:* for God had made them joyful with great joy ... and the joy of Jerusalem was heard afar off ... And they kept the watch of their God, and the observance of expiation, and *the singing men*, ... according to the commandment of David, and of Solomon his son. (45) For in the days of David and Asaph *from the beginning there were chief singers appointed, to praise with canticles,* and give thanks to

Music: Now and Then

God. (46) And *all Israel ... gave portions to the singing men ... day by day.*"

As usual, it was in misuse of God's bounty that men deviated from the paths of righteousness and justice. To take care of the portions given the singing men (II Esd. 13:4) a storehouse was set up: "And over this thing was Eliasib the priest, who was set over the treasury of the house of our God ... And he made him a great storeroom, where before him they laid up gifts, and frankincense, and vessels, and the tithes of the corn, of the wine, and of the oil, *the portions of the Levites and of the singing men*, and of the porters, and the first fruits of the priests." When Nehemias, who had been visiting Artaxerxes the King of Babylon, returned to Jerusalem, he (II Esd. 13:7) "understood the evil that Eliasib had done ... , to make him a storehouse in the courts of the house of God." Nehemias promptly "cleansed the storehouses," but (10) he "perceived that the portions of the Levites had not been given them: and that *the Levites, and the singing men*, and they that ministered were fled every man to his own country." And, in righteous wrath, Nehemias went before the magistrates, and said (11): "Why have we forsaken the house of God?" And Nehemias "gathered them togather ... and made them to stand in their places." Having obtained redress, he (13) appointed new keepers of the tithes, who "were approved as faithful, and to them were committed the portions of their brethren," including the Levites, and *"the singing men."* And Nehemias prayed (14): "Remember me, O my God, for this thing, and wipe not out my kindnesses, which I

Song, With Instruments

have done relating to the house of my God and his ceremonies."

Nehemias, in protesting the rights of "the Levites, and singing men," was as ruthless in righting wrongs of men, as he was faithful in observance of praise to God. On one occasion, as punishment for violation of the Sabbath, he related (II Esd. 13:25): "And I chid them (the malefactors), and laid my curse upon them, and shaved off their hair, and made them swear by God, that they would not continue in sin." Then Nehemias prayed (II Esd. 13:29–31): "Remember them, O Lord my God, that defile the priesthood, and the law of priests and Levites. So I separated from them all strangers (in purging for sins of concupiscence), and *I appointed the courses of the priests and the Levites, every man in his ministry:* And for the offering of wood at times appointed, and for the first fruits: remember me, O my God, unto good. Amen."

The building, rebuilding, restoring and dedication of altars for the worship of God were always accompanied by music, as we have seen. And, as we also know, musical performances were established and ordained as a tradition. In the maintenance of the tradition, however, we find much variety, both in use and deploying of singers, as well as in instruments. As late as 165 B.C., we read that Judas Machabeus, after the restoration of the sanctuary, "dedicated it (I Mach. 4:54) anew with *canticles, and harps, and lutes, and cymbals.*" This unmistakably indicates the existence of much variety, both of texture and timbre, in the late liturgical music of the Old Testament.

Music: Now and Then

In the book of Ecclesiasticus (50), Simon the high priest was vividly described (11) as being "clothed with the perfection of power" when "he put on the robe of glory" in the worship of God. (12) "When he went up to the holy altar, he honoured the vesture of holiness ... (13) And about him was a ring of his brethren ... (14) and all the sons of Aaron in their glory ... (18) *Then the sons of Aaron shouted, they sounded with beaten trumpets*, and made a great noise to be heard for a remembrance before God ... (20) *And the singers lifted up their voices, and in the great house the sound of sweet melody was increased.*"

The allusion to "melody" occurs again in Ecclesiasticus in a paean of praise and counsel (32:5–8): "Speak the first word with careful knowledge, and *hinder not music*. Where there is no hearing, pour not out words, and be not lifted up out of season with thy wisdom. *A concert of music* in a banquet of wine is as a carbuncle set in gold. As a signet of an emerald in a work of gold: so is the *melody of music* with pleasant and moderate wine." While this is unmistakably an injunction to "say it with music," rather than with an outpouring of words, there are two schools of thought on this subject.

Thomas a' Kempis (*Imitation of Christ*) warns against too great preoccupation with singing, at the expense of the "spiritual sense" of texts. First, praising musical simplicity and moderation in the observation: "*Simple music and moderate songs* touch sometimes the ear more pleasantly *than the swell of voices*, which break on the ear like peals of thunder, and fatigue rather than charm.

Song, With Instruments

Too bright lightning dazzles the eye: a moderate light keeps the vision in activity," and continues:

"I have seen simple souls bathed in tears in the fervour of prayer, while those who *sang with a loud and melodious voice*, felt nothing but dryness of heart... the simple... soul seeks only the glory of God... He ... attends seriously to *the spiritual sense* of the Psalms ... (he) *sings them with attention, taste*... Blessed is the *voice of him that sings* and declares *the praises of God* in such manner as to fill the hearts of those who hear him with compunction."

While Thomas a' Kempis awakens many responsive chords in the minds of those who have been exposed to much contemporary choral composition, the ancients seem to have possessed an uninhibited, lusty fondness for imposing musical effects on appropriate occasion. And, not unexpectedly, we find that when David brought "the ark of God... into the city with joy (II Kings 6:12)... *there were* with David *seven choirs*." This was, of course, in addition to instruments. As will be recalled, this was that special occasion, on which the spirit of improvisation was released in David, and he danced, with both happy and unhappy result. Even in our time, this is not an unfamiliar outcome of public performance, however. We recognize it as one of those frequent events, approved by the audience, but not meeting with critical favor; in this case the critic having been Michol, David's wife.

Music: Now and Then

◆§ Hymns, Psalms, and Canticles

For the purposes of this study, it is necessary to define the terms to be used, namely, "hymns," "psalms," and "canticles." It would indeed be a simple matter, at this point, paradoxically to become involved in the complexities of various tongues and translations, even of interpretations. But in order to keep a simple matter simple, we shall use the words "hymn," "canticle," and "psalm" in their most general, all-inclusive sense.

In early times, an act of praise to God, provided it was sung, was frequently termed a "hymn." The occasion need not have been, nor was it always, strictly liturgical, nor solely reserved for performance at fixed times by those duly appointed and ordained. However, it undoubtedly often partook of the character of instituted procedures and their essential spirit. A personal conclusion, arrived at from isolating and considering references to hymns from the time of Solomon to the first hymn mentioned in the annals of Christianity, is that participation occurred, generally, more freely and spontaneously, and that the "inspirational" spirit of a particular occasion was justification for hymn singing. Since our main consideration of the various uses of music throughout our investigations has been the motivating, illuminating spirit of the various occasions discussed, we shall avoid technical and speculative considerations, which may readily come to mind, such as the first introduction of metrical hymns, etc. Though metrical hymns were introduced in the Christian era by

Hymns, Psalms, and Canticles

St. Ambrose, perpetuated by Gregory the Great, followed by St. Benedict, it cannot be assumed that they did not exist long before, and that their roots did not extend deeply into the period antedating the coming of Christ.

When Solomon (III Kings 8:28) offered up prayers, at the time of the assembling of the people for the dedication of the temple, it was in the manner of a spontaneous outpouring, in song, with (54) "both knees on the ground and hands spread towards heaven:" "O Lord my God: *hear the hymn* and the prayer, which thy servant prayeth before thee this day:" And from verses 29 to 53 follows one of the most inspired supplications to the Almighty in all the Bible. That it was purely inspirational in character and specially timed for a moment of divine communication is evident. And it was even at the Last Supper, that Christ and his disciples (Matt. 26:30, and Mark 14:26), following the first Holy Eucharist, paused, "and *a hymn being said*, they went out into mount Olivet."

Although few words were given to this simple statement, it required no descriptive eloquence. But its profound significance is unmistakable. That Jesus Christ, the Son of God, paused to offer a hymn to God the Father at the most divine and fateful moment in the history of humanity, possesses a profundity of meaning to which nothing may add — nor can anything take away.

When David was inspired to "bring again the ark of our God" to the Israelites from Cariathiarim (I Par. 13) *he* (8) "*and all Israel played* before God with all

Music: Now and Then

their might *with hymns*, and *with harps*, and *with psalteries*, and *timbrels*, and *cymbals*, and *trumpets*." This was one of those mass demonstrations dear to the heart of David. The singing of hymns, with imposing instrumental support, presumably in open spaces, is in marked contrast to the performance of liturgical music, within the confines of the tabernacle, or other duly appointed places and occasions. And it will be noted that "all Israel," not merely the "singing men," participated.

From what we already know of David's interest in music, not only in performance but in its institution as an essential concomitant of worship, in regular liturgy, as well as in unforeseen moments when the spirit moved him, it is clear that his influence is without parallel in musical annals. While much of his musical expression was inspirational, peculiar to him and incapable of repetition or being formalized into traditional procedure, David was responsible for musical ordinances and influences that have continued, as we have seen, even to modern times.

So we read (II Par. 7), after the death of David, when Solomon dedicated the temple which he had built "to the name of the Lord," (6) "the priests stood in their offices: and *the Levites with the instruments of music of the Lord*, which King David *made to praise the Lord:* because his mercy endureth forever, *singing the hymns of David by their ministry:* and *the priests sounded with trumpets* before them, and all Israel stood."

As we have already observed, it was David's spirit of fantasy, of extemporaneousness, that seized the

Hymns, Psalms, and Canticles

imagination and inflamed the spirit of the nineteenth-century composer, Robert Schumann. While Schumann acknowledged this debt in the formation of the *Davidsbund*, and other specific tributes to David's influence, it cannot be said that the great French composer, Hector Berlioz, made similar acknowledgment. Yet, is it not manifest that Berlioz' predilection for extravagant orchestral combinations and effects may have had their source in David's bold experiments in the mass, diversified assemblage of instruments, with choirs?

At the laying of the foundations of the temple by Josue, (I Esd. 3:10), "when the masons laid the foundations ... (11) *they* (the priests with trumpets, and the Levites, etc.) *sung together hymns*, and *praise to the Lord:* because he is good, for his mercy endureth forever towards Israel. And all the people shouted with a great shout, praising the Lord, because the foundations of the temple of the Lord were laid." Again, the celebration seems to have been spontaneous, and everyone within earshot was caught up by the occasion, *"singing together hymns"* in praise of the Almighty.

References to hymns in connection with battle were rare in Biblical times, but not more so than in the days of the "Battle Hymn of the Republic." Exceptions are to be found at the time of Judas Machabeus (I Mach. 4:24, etc.) both in praise for the defeat of Gorgias, when, *"returning home they sung a hymn*, and blessed God in heaven, because he is good, because his mercy endureth forever,"* and, later, when the Israelites were attacked by Lysias (165 B.C.). In the latter instance, before battle, in supplication to God for the destruc-

Music: Now and Then

tion of the enemy, Judas Machabeus did not fail to conclude his prayer with a note of praise (33): "Cast them (the enemy) down with the sword of them that love thee: and let all that know thy name, *praise thee with hymns.*" It is worthy of note that Judas Machabeus praised God both before and after battle. Faith in God-given victory was implicit, even in the midst of entreaty for the confounding of the enemy.

Simon, the successor to Judas Machabeus, likewise used hymns in praise of the Almighty, as at the fall of Gaza (143 B.C.). When the enemy, defeated, under Simon's leadership, by the Israelites, were spared, "Simon being moved" (I Mach. 13:47), he "cast them out of the city . . . cleansed the houses . . . and then he entered into it *with hymns,* blessing the Lord." Later, Simon (142 B.C.), having recaptured the castle at Jerusalem, (50) thrown out the enemy, and "cleansed the castle from uncleanness . . . (51) entered into it *with thanksgiving,* and branches of palm trees, and *harps,* and *cymbals* and *psalteries,* and *hymns,* and *canticles,* because the great enemy was destroyed out of Israel. (52) And *he ordained that these days should be kept every year* with gladness." Simon was indeed a worthy follower of David both in the lavishness and extemporaneousness of this musical celebration, and in establishing it as a memorial to be preserved: as a tradition.

More in the manner of an ordained religious ceremonial was the singing of hymns (II Mach. 1:30), at the time of Nehemias offered prayer and sacrifice to God: "And *the priests sung hymns* till the sacrifice was consumed." Truer to the traditional use of hymns on occa-

Hymns, Psalms, and Canticles

sions not connected with liturgical worship, was the celebration of the capture of Gazara by the Israelites under Judas, when "they (II Mach. 10:38) *blessed the Lord with hymns and thanksgiving*, who had done great things in Israel, and given them the victory."

However, as we noted before, Judas Machabeus did not reserve his praise of God merely for celebration of victory. In the very midst of battle (II Mach. 12:36), when they "had fought long, and were weary, Judas called upon the Lord ... (37): Then beginning *in his own language*, and *singing hymns with a loud voice*, he put Gorgias' soldiers to flight." The victory, accompanied by music, is strongly reminiscent of the fall of Jericho. However, let it be noted that the cumulative, physical power of mass, instrumental sound, in case of Jericho, was superseded (163 B.C.), at the date so much closer to the Christian era, by the more spiritual force of the human voice, with specifically mentioned language.

. . . . .

In the time of the Apostles (Acts 16:24, 25), when Paul and Silas, in prison with "their feet fast in the stocks ... praying, *praised God*, and they that were in prison, heard them," this was unquestionably an early example of Christian hymnology. That hymn singing was a custom to be cherished and preserved is implicit in St. Paul's admonition (Eph. 5:18, 19): "And be ye not drunk with wine, wherein is luxury; but be ye filled with the holy Spirit, Speaking to yourselves in *psalms* and *hymns*, and *spiritual canticles*, *singing and making melody* in your hearts to the Lord." The analogy of the inebriation resulting from both wine drinking and singing is unmistakable, the essential difference lying in the spirituous reaction of the one, and the spiritual elevation of the other!

Similar exhortation is to be found in St. Paul's epistle to the Colossians (Col. 3:16): "Let the word of Christ dwell in you abundantly, in all wisdom: teaching and admonishing one another *in psalms, hymns, and spiritual canticles, singing* in grace in your hearts to God."

The occasional references to canticles, sometimes singly, but often in the same breath as "hymns" and "psalms," denote a difference in meaning and usage. Again, the danger of over-simplification is manifest, but that of obscuring our purposes is even greater. So we shall leave to the infinite number of researchists, translators, musicologists, *et al.*, all quibbling and minutiae in their various and varied definitions of the term. For our purposes, we must be content with regarding a "canticle" as a mystical song, frequently prophetic, embodying the mystical union of Christ and the Church. The canticle is our musical holy of holies! If taken literally, the canticle remains inexplicable. If one is inducted, through meditation in the manner of St. Bernard, into its mysteries, the canticle possesses an enhaloed significance, not to be desecrated by vain probings. The union of the Church with God, although sung in the imagery of human love, was a source of poetic and musical inspiration, mystical in nature, not associated to the same degree with either "hymns," or "psalms," although, at times, the line of demarcation, especially with the latter, is scarcely to be perceived.

Hymns, Psalms, and Canticles

Allegory is the human investiture of the canticle; its essential spirit is mystical!

Passing references to canticles have already been made occasionally, if infrequently, in these pages. To draw these widely dispersed references into a pattern would serve no new purpose. However, it seems most pertinent, at this point, to reconsider the deeply inspired words of St. Bernard of Clairvaux on the greatest of all canticles, namely, those of Solomon (trans. of Terence L. Connolly, S.J.): "You must not think that there is no significance in the fact that the title of this Book (Solomon's) is not simply a 'Canticle' but the 'Canticle of Canticles.' Many, indeed, are the canticles which I have read in Holy Scriptures and no one of them do I remember as being called by such a title. Israel sang a song to the Lord because it had escaped both the sword and the yoke of Pharaoh, by the twofold service of the sea, marvelously delivered and at the same time avenged. Yet what it sang was not called the 'Canticle of Canticles,' but, if I remember rightly, Israel, says the Scripture, *sang this Canticle to the Lord.* Deborah also sang a song, and Judith sang a song, and the mother of Samuel sang a song (I Kings 2), some of the prophets also sang a song, and no one of these, as we read, called his song the 'Canticle of Canticles' . . . But the famous King, Solomon, singular in wisdom, exalted in fame, having an abundance of material things, secure in peace, is known to have had need of nothing such as, received, would have led him to repeat that song of his. Nor does his own writing seem anywhere to suggest any such thing. And so it was under divine inspiration that he sang the praises of Christ and the Church, the grace of holy love, and the mysteries of marriage eternal. At the same time he expressed the longing of a saintly soul and composed a nuptial song exulting in spirit, in delightful but figurative language ... Therefore, I believe, it is because of its very excellence that this nuptial song is distinguished beyond all others by the title, 'Canticle of Canticles,' just as He to whom that song is sung is alone called, King of Kings and Lord of lords.

"It is a canticle that is itself the fruit of all the rest. The anointing of grace alone can teach a canticle of this sort: experience only can unfold its meaning. Let those who have had experience of it recognize it: let those inexperienced in it burn with a longing not so much of knowing as of actually experiencing it. For, it is not a noise of the mouth, but a shout of the heart: not a sound of the lips, but a tumult of internal delights: a harmony of wills, not of voices. It is not heard outside, for it does not cry out in public. (Keats: 'Heard melodies are sweet, but those unheard are sweeter.') Only the one who sings hears it, and the one for whom it is sung, that is, the Bridegroom and the bride. For it is a nuptial song expressing the chaste and joyous embrace of souls, the harmony of their behavior, the blending of their affections in mutual charity." (St. Bernard on the Love of God, Connally, Abbey of Gethsemani, Kentucky.)

Although the mystical significance of the "canticle" was not always implicit, either in the occasion or manner of expression, it became increasingly so with the

Hymns, Psalms, and Canticles

approach of and after the advent of Christ. And, in spite of Solomon's having sung the "Canticle of Canticles" with divine "remembrance of things to come," it is not until we come to the supernatural, revelations of St. John that the greatest heights and depths of the canticle, as prophecy of the mystical union of the soul and the infinity of God's spirit, are opened up to us. (Apoc. 5): "And I saw in the right hand of him that sat on the throne (4:'he ... was to the sight like the jasper and the sardine stone: and there was a rainbow round about the throne, in sight like unto an emerald'), a book written within and without, sealed with seven seals. And I saw a strong angel, proclaiming with a loud voice: Who is worthy to open the book, and to loose the seals thereof? And no man was able, neither in heaven, nor on earth, nor under the earth, to open the book, nor to look on it. And I wept much, because no man was found worthy to open the book, nor to see it. And one of the ancients (of the 'four and twenty ancients' sitting about the throne) said to me: Weep not; behold the lion of the tribe of Juda, the root of David, hath prevailed to open the book, and to loose the seven seals thereof. And I saw: and behold in the midst of the throne and of the four living creatures ('full of eyes before and behind ... the first ... like a lion, the second ... like a calf, the third having the face, as it were, of a man: and the fourth living creature was like an eagle flying ... they rested not day and night, saying: Holy, holy, holy, Lord God Almighty, who was, and who is, and who is to come'), and in the midst of the ancients, a Lamb standing as it were slain, having seven horns

Music: Now and Then

and seven eyes: which are the seven Spirits of God, sent forth into all the earth. And he came and took the book out of the right hand of him that sat on the throne. And when he opened the book, the four living creatures, and the four and twenty ancients fell down before the Lamb, *having every one of them harps*, and golden viols full of odours, which are the prayers of the saints: *And they sung a new canticle*, saying: Thou are worthy, O Lord, to take the book, and to open the seals thereof; because thou was slain, and has redeemed us to God, in thy blood ... And the four and twenty ancients fell down on their faces, and adored him that liveth for ever and ever."

Following other mystical visions, St. John wrote (Apoc. 14): (1) "And I beheld, and lo a lamb stood upon mount Sion, and with him an hundred forty-four thousand, having his name, and the name of his Father, written on their foreheads. (2) And I heard a voice from heaven, as the noise of many waters, and as the voice of great thunder; and the voice which I heard, was *as the voice of harpers, harping on their harps*. (3) And they sung as it were *a new canticle*, before the throne, and before the four living creatures, and the ancients; and *no man could say the canticle, but those hundred forty-four thousand*, who were purchased from the earth ... (4) These follow the Lamb whithersoever he goeth. These were purchased from among men, the first fruits to God and to the Lamb. (5) And in their mouth there was found no lie; for they are without spot before the throne of God."

In the midst of the fearful and wonderful things that St. John envisioned, the most sacred moments were in-

Hymns, Psalms, and Canticles

tensified in their exaltation of the Almighty by music: *a new canticle* glorifying God, and uniting the pure in heart with Him forever. (Apoc. 15): (2) "And I saw as it were a sea of glass mingled with fire, and them that had overcome the beast, and his image, and the number of his name, standing on the sea of glass, having *the harps of God:* (3) And singing the canticle of Moses, the servant of God, and the *canticle of the Lamb*, saying: Great and wonderful are thy works, O Lord God Almighty; just and true are thy ways, O King of ages."

The vision of singing around the throne of God inspired Thomas a' Kempis (*Imitation of Christ*) to exclaim with celestial ecstasy and divine aspiration: "O Lord, when shall I hear *the voice of Thy praise* from the lips of Thine Angels in heaven; as the blessed Apostle John . . . heard the *voices of many Angels singing* together, 'Holy, Holy, Holy?' *O that I were with them and had such a voice.** Gladly would I praise Thee with them; and above *the most exalted canticles* in heaven *sing and magnify Thy holy name forever!* O Cherubim and Seraphim, how sweetly and well, how fervently and excellently do ye *sing and give jubilee before God*, free from all meanness and fatigue, and without ceasing in everlasting felicity. *Wherefore every human voice sounds hoarse to me; all songs discordant; all psalmody

---

* Vide E. A. Poe's *Israfel:*
"If I could dwell where Israfel
Hath dwelt, and he where I,
He might not sing so wildly well
A mortal melody,
While a bolder note than this might swell
From my lyre within the sky."

Music: Now and Then

dry; all music burthenous; every harp unstrung; every instrument out of tune ... yea, all things nothing *in comparison with eternal life, eternal glory, eternal joy, in the sight of God and his Angels, who in most exalted song ever give praise to the Holy and Glorious Trinity, day and night forever.* But because I cannot ascend to *those sublime Canticles of the Heavens,* nor am fully able to comprehend them, therefore I mourn over myself and mightily despise myself, and bend my knees before God, and all men, and humbly crave pardon. For verily all my works are nothing without Thee ... For *Thou art my music and harp, my organ and timbrel, O my God! Thou art the psalm that brings gladness to my heart, my canticle, and my song of joy, O my God!*"

. . . . .

Biblical music is commonly associated with "psalms," and this appears to be a natural outgrowth from the various original, all-inclusive words from which the one title, "psalms" is derived, whether the scriptural version be Hebrew, Greek or Vulgate. The spirit of the occasions for singing in worship of God, whether in psalms, hymns or canticles, is best described in the familiar injunction of St. Paul to the Ephesians (5:18, 19): "be ye filled with the holy Spirit, Speaking to yourselves *in psalms, and hymns, and spiritual canticles, singing and making melody in your hearts to the Lord.*" No matter what the particular character of a *psalm*, in praise, prophecy, prayer or penitence, glorification of God is the design of them all. In addition to their all-embracing spiritual nature, their outstanding char-

Hymns, Psalms, and Canticles

acteristic is that they were *songs accompanied by an instrument,* in all probability, *most frequently the harp.*

We have already encountered David's various musical exploits, those of skill and extemporization, as well as of ordinance. But the crowning glory of David's extraordinary accomplishments and versatility, rests eternally on the Psalms, the majority of which were of his composition. The poet Wordsworth most aptly termed the Psalms "A spiritual epitome of all history." While no written words in the annals of mankind are more generally known or profound in their influence than those of the Psalms, their music, as far as concrete evidence goes, is regarded by many as a closed book. At best, it is considered to be a highly speculative matter. It is, nevertheless, reasonable to review briefly for a moment, the recorded beginnings, ordinance and preservation, through tradition, of music throughout the ages, and make fresh inquiry into the fancied, rather than real, lapse of that tradition in the very beginnings of the Christian era, with regard to the Psalms.

From the scriptural text, we have already had evidence of musical beginnings, perpetuation, from father to son, organization, for battle and other purposes, ordination as an essential part of worship, as well as other manifold usages and developments. However, it must be remembered that what appear as beginnings are, in reality, culminating peaks in a natural sequence of evolutionary changes. These points of attainment only are recorded, in accounts that seldom make any attempt to depict the gradual ascent to the summit. For instance, when Jubal is first mentioned in Genesis as the

Music: Now and Then

"father of them who played ...," reason tells us that he was not the initial musical progenitor, but the one appointed to organize and perpetuate, to establish as tradition, something that had been taking shape over an uncertain period of time. For even in the scriptures, at times, "a thousand years were but as a day."

Similarly, the musical ordinances that appear in scriptural texts, were dominating peaks, looming on the horizon, with no attempt made to record intervening changes and developments. What appears on the visible surface of Biblical, historical annals, presupposes an unperceived (from a far-removed vantage point), continuous musical undercurrent, from the earliest times, through the Christian era. Only in this way can one logically explain the emergence (for such it was) of plain song, Gregorian chant and all musical changes of early Christianity.

It would, therefore, be unreasonable to assume, inasmuch as instituted musical procedures in the worship of God by the Israelites, existing as tradition through many hundreds of years, were not continued in full glory by the earliest Christians, that the tradition vanished from the face of the earth. Traditions had been maintained in many earlier periods, in which the duration of time spans are less certain to us, and it would indeed be most illogical to conclude that they vanished in the relatively short space of time between the coming of Christ and the development of the Church into an organized establishment, with smoothly functioning liturgical, musical office. Hence, the assumption that traditional musical renditions, even of the Psalms,

Hymns, Psalms, and Canticles

stemming from David, were continued, is logical. Like a stream, apparent to the eye at one moment, but continuing its unbroken if unperceived course, underground, the next, so even the Apostles, wherever they came together, prayed and sang: as St. Paul wrote (I Cor. 14:15): "I will pray with the spirit, I will pray also with the understanding; *I will sing with the spirit, I will sing also with the understanding.*" And St. Paul continued with the injunction (26): "When you are come together, *everyone of you hath a psalm*, hath a revelation, hath a tongue, hath an interpretation: let all things be done to edification." Although the early Christians did not worship always in the orderly and ordained surroundings of duly appointed houses of worship, the power of the Holy Spirit was in nowise lessened in them, and they sang with the "spirit" as well as "understanding." And, whenever or wherever they came together, everyone of them had a "psalm," to "edification." The promise to God by Ezechias was thus kept by the early Christians, and the long-established tradition clearly maintained (Isaias 38:20): "O Lord, save me, and *we will sing our psalms all the days of our life* in the house of the Lord."

Much that is authoritative and inspired has been written on the Psalms, from St. Augustine to our own day. For the purposes of this record, nothing additional may be added to their consideration or elucidation. We are merely concerned with their intimate relationship to music, with which, in conception and purpose, they were indissolubly linked. As for the appreciation and understanding of the Psalms, themselves, if we would

Music: Now and Then

"taste the honey of God" we must "have the palate of faith." "Attune thy heart to the psalm. *If the psalm prays, pray thou; if it mourns, mourn thou; if it fears, fear thou.* Everything, in the psalter, is the looking glass of the soul." (St. Augustine) "Vita sic canta, ut nunquam sileas."

Throughout the Psalms, direct references are made to music, both in given directions and in the body of the text. The commonest musical direction is the much-debated word "Selah," which occurs seventy-one times. It is derived from *shelah*, "rest," and is a music mark denoting a pause, during which the singers ceased to sing and only the accompanying instruments were heard. Selah was used not merely where the sense required a rest, but to afford a moment of calm reflection on the preceding words. In order to induce contemplation, the selah reminds that the psalm requires a peaceful and meditative soul that can apprehend what the Holy Spirit propounds. It is far from being a superfluous indication, as some have contended. Both the musical and psychological import of "selah" are not to be disregarded. Such values were sensed later, in the song writing of Schumann, for instance, when an instrumental section, alone, provided an interlude or postlude, after words of peculiar significance, to give added emphasis, or pause for contemplation.

There are frequent dedications of psalms "to the chief musician:" to whom, it is supposed, they were given to be sung and played. Psalm 6, the first penitential psalm, has a foreword: "a psalm of David, *for the octave.*" This was probably meant to be sung with an

Hymns, Psalms, and Canticles

instrument of eight strings. St. Augustine, however, "understands it mystically, of the last resurrection and the world to come; which is, as it were, the octave, or eighth day, after the seven days of this mortal life; and for this octave, sinners must dispose themselves, like David, by bewailing their sins, whilst they are here upon earth." The notation, "for the octave," appears again before Psalm 11.

In addition to the "octave," another musical instrument is mentioned in connection with Psalm 8: "for the presses" (Hebrew "Gittith"), also Maeleth, or Machalath (Ps. 52), although the dedication of so many of the Psalms to specified "musicians" and "chief musicians," as well as David's musical directions and known predilection for instrumental usage, indicate beyond a doubt that instruments normally supported and extended the singing of the Psalms. Even the texts are filled with the spirit of song, not only in poetic imagery and rhythm, but in such references (Ps. 12) as: "My heart shall rejoice in thy salvation: *I will sing to the Lord*, who giveth me good things; yea *I will sing to Lord most high.*" Similarly, (Ps. 20): "*We will sing* and praise thy power." Some of the Psalms, in consonance with their all-pervading spirit, are "canticles," full of profound mystery and the sanctity of Christ: a "*canticle* to him in the night" (Ps. 41:9), even "Unto the end, for them that shall be changed ... for understanding. A *canticle for the Beloved*," viz., Our Lord Jesus Christ.

In the Psalms, truly the voice of the Almighty is carried on wings of song (Ps. 46:6–8): "*God is ascended with jubilee, and the Lord with the sound of trumpet. Sing*

Music: Now and Then

praises to our God, sing ye: sing praises to our King, sing ye. For God is the King of all the earth: *sing ye wisely.*"

The reasons ascribed by David for singing the praises of the Lord are as diversified and endless as God's bounty to him (Ps. 58:17–19): "*I will sing* thy strength: and will extol thy mercy in the morning. For thou art become my support, and my refuge, in the day of my trouble. *Unto thee, O my helper, will I sing,* for thou art God my defense: my God my mercy." (Ps. 60:8, 9): "His mercy and truth who shall search? So *I will sing a psalm* to thy name *forever and ever:* that I may pay my vows from day to day." Not only Sion, but all the earth was called upon by David to sing praises. (Ps. 64:2): "*A hymn,* O God, *becometh thee* in Sion," (Ps. 65:1, 2. 4): "*Shout with joy to God, all the earth. Sing ye a psalm to his name; give glory to his praise . . . Let all the earth adore thee, and sing to thee; let it sing a psalm to thy name.*"

The idea implicit in the phrase: "*give glory* to his praise" (by singing the psalm) is identical with that expressed by Edgar Allan Poe in his essay on the "Poetic Principle," in which Poe expounds the relationship of words and music. It is indicated beyond a doubt that David recognized that the *appropriate union of music and text* added "glory" to words of praise. Indeed, the might of David's tremendous pronouncements was increased by raising the voice in song (Ps. 67:33, 34): "*Sing ye to God,* ye Kingdoms of the earth: *sing ye to the Lord: Sing ye to God,* who mounteth above the heaven of heavens, . . . *Behold he will give his voice the voice of power.*"

Hymns, Psalms, and Canticles

A notable reference to the ancient ordination of music, quite different from David's plenitude of extemporaneous outpourings in song, is found in Asaph's Psalm, "for the winepresses," (Ps. 80:2-6): "Rejoice to God our helper: *sing aloud to the God of Jacob. Take a psalm, and bring hither the timbrel: the pleasant psaltery with the harp. Blow up the trumpet on the new moon, on the noted day of your solemnity. For it is a commandment in Israel, and a judgment to the God of Jacob. He ordained it for a testimony* in Joseph, when he came out of the land of Egypt: *he heard a tongue which he knew not.*" In the midst of strangers, whose language was not understood, music was the natural God-given medium of expression, bringing peoples of diverse tongues together on common meeting ground: through the *universal experience of music*, and was specifically ordained for this purpose! That the singing of Psalms was instituted in perpetuity, is again manifest in Ps. 88:2 "The mercies of the Lord *I will sing forever.*"

Delight in lifting the voice in song, the experience of spiritual elevation, are to be derived from the singing of Psalms (Ps. 91:2-4): "It is *good* to give praise to the Lord: *and to sing to thy name:* O most High. To shew forth thy mercy in the morning, and thy truth in the night: *Upon an instrument of ten strings, upon the psaltery: with a canticle upon the harp.*" Not only is such spiritual elevation to be derived from praising God in song, but it is found as a preliminary injunction from David (Ps. 94:1, 2): "Come let us praise the Lord with joy: let us joyfully sing to God our saviour. *Let us come before his presence with thanksgiving; and make a joyful*

Music: Now and Then

noise to him with psalms." Again (Ps. 99:2, 4): *"Sing joyfully to God, all the earth: serve ye the Lord with gladness. Come in before his presence with exceeding great joy ... Go ye into his gates with praise, into his courts with hymns: and give glory to him."* Not only joy, but the gift of understanding was to be derived from the singing of psalms (Ps. 100:1, 2): *"Mercy and judgment I will sing to thee, O Lord: I will sing, and I will understand in the unspotted way ..."*

All of the Psalms are evidence of man's faith in and dependence upon the Almighty, expressed in unparalleled words, glorified in music. If, in the first days of the Christian era, some of the fullness of their expression was lost, in the midst of the vicissitudes of the early followers of Christ, the quickening spirit which inspired the psalms was and is as unceasing and everlasting as the infinity of the Almighty. It is only the human manifestations of this spirit, even in music, that, at times, have and will fail, even today.

The group of fifteen psalms, beginning with Psalm 69, known as "Graduals," has been the subject of much research and various interpretations. That these Psalms had to do with ascending steps, is indubitable. Whether the steps were real or symbolic, or both, is a point of discussion. In the circumstances, we can only consider the various points of view, mainly speculative, and express a preference. The Rev. A. R. Fausset, evidently an Anglican clergyman, writes in his critical and expository encyclopaedia: "Pilgrim songs: four by David, one by Solomon, ten anonymous, from: *shir hama'-aloth*, 'a song for the ascendings,' *i.e.*, for the *going up*

Hymns, Psalms, and Canticles

(Jerusalem and its temple being regarded as on a moral *elevation* above other places, as it was in fact on the most elevated tableland of the country, requiring a *going up* from all sides) to the three great feasts ... The simple style, brevity and transitions formed by retaining a word from the previous verse ('whence *cometh my help, my help cometh*') are suitable to pilgrim-song poetry ... "

The approved (by Leo XIII, Dec. 13, 1898) Douay version of the Bible has the following notation: "*A gradual canticle* (at Ps. 119): The following psalms, in number fifteen, are called *the gradual psalms*, or *canticles*, from the word *gradus*, signifying steps, ascensions or degrees: either because they were appointed to be sung on the *fifteen steps*, by which the people *ascended* to the temple: or, that, in the singing of them the voice was to be raised by certain *steps* or *ascensions;* or, that they were to be sung by the people returning from their captivity and *ascending* to Jerusalem, which was seated amongst the mountains. The holy fathers, in a mystical sense, understand these steps, or ascensions, of the degrees by which Christians spiritually ascend to virtue and perfection; and to the true temple of God in the heavenly Jerusalem."

From a musicological viewpoint, the idea that "in the singing of them the voice was to be raised by certain steps or ascensions," is of prime importance. Since we cannot all be musicologists, but should and must attach the greatest significance to inner, spiritual meanings, the conception of the gradual rises "by which Christians ascend to virtue and perfection" strikes

Music: Now and Then

with greater force and conviction. Fortunately, the various points of view are not actually in conflict, and none precludes acceptance and belief in a deeper, spiritual significance, which is certainly implicit throughout the Psalms.

The promise of singing to God without ceasing is continued to the final Psalms (Ps. 145:2): "Praise the Lord, O my soul, in my life I will praise the Lord: *I will sing to my God as long as I shall be,*" because (Ps. 146:1) "*psalm is good:* to our God be joyful and comely praise," (Ps. 148:13, 14): "for his name alone is exalted, The praise of him is above heaven and earth ... *A hymn to all his saints: to the children of Israel, a people approaching to him.* Alleluia." (Ps. 149:1-3) "*Sing ye to the Lord a new canticle:* let his praise be in the church of the saints. Let Israel rejoice in him that made him: and let the children of Sion be joyful to their King. Let them *praise his name in choir:* let them *sing to him with the timbrel and the psaltery.*"

And, finally, the inspired order of the Psalms brings us to a climax of power and praise, appropriately cumulative (Ps. 150), the overwhelming *Laudate Dominum in sanctus:* "Praise ye the Lord in his holy places: praise him in the firmament of his power. Praise him for his mighty acts: praise him according to the multitude of his greatness. *Praise him with the sound of trumpet:* praise him *with the psaltery and the harp.* Praise him *with the timbrel and choir:* praise him *with strings and organs.* Praise him *on high sounding cymbals:* praise him *on cymbals of joy:* LET EVERY SPIRIT PRAISE THE LORD. ALLELUIA."